The Cat Who Sang
& Other Stories of Rescued Animals

Katie's Place
Animal Shelter

Phone: 604-463-7917

Email: katies.place@shaw.ca

Shelter address:
10255 Jackson Road, Maple Ridge
Open Hours: Sat & Sun, noon-2:00

Mailing address:
20803 Camwood Avenue,
Maple Ridge, B.C. V2X 2N9

Petfinder at www.katiesplace.petfinder.com
or Adopt-a-Pet (www.adoptapet.com)

Charitable Registration Number:
86250 6037 RR0001

Please note – Katie's Place is full and is only able to
accept new animals by referral.

Library and Archives Canada Data
Entered under title:
The Cat Who Sang and Other Stories of Rescued Animals
(Pets/General)

ISBN
978-0-9813528-0-0

Copywrite © 2009, Brigitta MacMillan
All rights reserved

Printing costs paid by a volunteer.
All proceeds to Katie's Place's vet bills.

Our heartfelt thanks go to Robert Saunders who donated his skills to design the cover, to Ashley O'Mara of Ashleycakes who designed the graphic on page 4, to the people who contributed to editing and getting the book into print, and to our supporters for caring about small souls who had nobody left to care.

*Dedicated to our beloved animals
and the people who care about them.*

5

*"When I think of the many cats all over that are going to be put down today for less....
Lovable, well-behaved cats with nothing worse than URI are at risk right now," wrote the volunteer, "I wonder if this hopeless case is worth agonizing over. It's like searching for a lost grain of salt when the entire salt shaker has spilled."*

*"We only deal with the single lost grains,"
Carol replied, "we cannot deal with the whole thing. So Keiko is fully worth our efforts. We make no judgment on whose life is worth saving and whose life is not. If we know, we acknowledge and take action if we can."*

Contents

8

Preface

People find themselves owned by their pet as much as they own them. Animals move into our homes and negotiate a relationship. They let us know what they like to eat, where they want to sleep, and what they like to do. Whether they get what they want depends on whose will is stronger, and some people capitulate to their pets – always laughingly, always with love. Living with pets is a partnership between human and animal. But it's not an equal partnership. It's a partnership in which we humans maintain ultimate control.

The bottom line is that we can get rid of them without raising an eyebrow among our neighbours if a pet becomes too demanding or inconvenient. They are, in fact, a body of persons without rights. Even that is changing as advocates plead for recognition of animals' rights under the law. Animal advocacy is a field as charged with passion as animal rescue. The reason is the animals themselves. We discover ourselves in them. Their pain is our pain, and their relief is our relief. We cannot know them without being moved by them.

Rescuers find themselves drawn deeply and irrevocably into a relationship with animals that can never be the same as it was before we became rescuers. When our first grubby, snarling stray recovers enough to reveal his self, we are changed. At first, we can't picture this slashing beast as ever welcoming human contact, either in his past or in the future. Then, in an oft-repeated story, a guarded, unknowable face one day takes on a softer aspect with a questioning look. If we extend a tentative hand, it's met by a tentative muzzle reaching back. Once they take us into their confidence, we can see what they've been through. Now their full grief and pain lie bare in their eyes. We can recognize the unquestioning faith they had in the people who loved them at their birth, and their confusion when the love was suddenly gone. We can see what it means to them to be loved again. Their gestures and their eyes are more eloquent than words. Over time, we come to know them intimately, and it turns out that they are more like us than we ever dreamed.

The more animals we meet and the longer we know them, the more we realize they're as complex and as individual as we are in their capacity for compassion, humour, embarrassment... for anything we ourselves experience. Where they differ from humans is in their vulnerability. They depend on us for their lives and, moreover, they trust us. That's where passions become inflamed. Nothing cuts like the betrayal of trust.

The story each animal tells is different according to his personality and his past, but we resonate with each story as fellow living beings. It's not something we can really explain to others. We can only hope to show them with the stories of a few of the souls we've been privileged to know.

This book is about animals who have changed the lives of their rescuers and of their adopters.

Introduction

Volunteering in animal rescue creeps up on you. It's not something you do all at once. Volunteers usually start by adopting. They venture nervously into a shelter, shielding their eyes from sad faces, and they pick out an animal while aching for all those they can't take. Many of these adopters get in touch later, "Do you need blankets or food?" Some come back to do a shift cleaning or feeding for a few months. A few stay for years. They take more animals home, and they get involved with the running of the shelter. For a few of these people, animal rescue becomes their life's work. Spouses and children deal with a whole new presence in the family as the shelter takes on a persona of its own.

So it was for the first volunteers of Katie's Place. They each had a couple of pets of their own. Then they began helping out at their local shelter. Then they looked after a few homeless cats they kept in a barn which was already home to a curmudgeonly cat named Katie. The population in the barn grew until it became the shelter called Katie's Place. The volunteers watched with pride and amazement as it became a sizable, permanent and well-regarded facility.

Katie's Place is completely volunteer run to this day. None of us meant to start a shelter. Those first animal lovers just needed a place to keep a half dozen cats until adopters could be found. They put the word out and found adopters – and more cats. The number of desperate, unwanted animals is so great that the barn was full within the first year. The barn had already taken the name, "Katie's Place," for a newsletter distributed to attract donors and adopters. The Maple Ridge Pitt Meadows Times began to feature Katie's Place animals on a monthly adoption page, and the volunteers began posting their pets on Petfinder.com.

The thirty-four cats in the barn by 2002 were soon joined by a dozen feral rabbits, rescued from the grounds of an institution that had been ready to exterminate them. A sheep, which was fished out of the Fraser River, lived in the front office for a couple of weeks before going to live out her life on a hobby farm. Several other small animals arrived over time, pet rats, guinea pigs, a pair of budgies, chickens... but the vast majority were cats. The volunteers narrowed their admission criteria when the barn was full and accepted last-hope cases. If there were options for a cat, callers were advised of them when their cat was declined.

The policy of giving priority to last-hope cases made Katie's Place exceptional. These animals are the elderly, the ill or injured, and traumatized animals who lash out in anger or fear. They can be costly to keep when they need extensive veterinary care or cannot be adopted out. They are animals who would have been put down elsewhere. The volunteers were moved by their hopelessness and accepted them out of compassion, acting from 'heart' alone. It could have been the shelter's undoing. Meeting veterinary costs would be a hurdle.

And a barn full of unadoptable animals would mean no room for further last-hope cases. They acted on faith and, to the surprise of any realists among them, their faith was vindicated. It seems that the public was also moved by these hopeless cases. Donations were always enough to pay the shelter's veterinary bills in full each year.

Veterinary costs exploded with the policy of giving last-chance animals priority. The volunteers paid $13,757 in vet bills for 2001. By 2008, the yearly vet bill was $66,277. As for the animals, their injuries healed, illnesses were cured, and most went on to new homes. Timid or aggressive animals were the greatest surprise when most of them became cheerful and affectionate, given time for their hurt to heal. These too found new homes. Elderly cats and cats with Feline Immunodeficiency Virus (FIV) or Feline Leukemia went out as permanent fosters when places could be found. Katie's Place retained responsibility for vet bills while the cat gained a home and a family gained a loving pet. This freed space in the shelter for more animals. There were always just enough volunteers to look after all the animals and just enough money to meet their costs.

In 2004, Katie's Place incorporated. In April 2005, the shelter became a registered charity. In November 2005, the people who loaned us the barn and saw a shelter mushroom on their doorstep gave notice that they wanted their barn back. The challenge of finding a new site and building a new shelter would span three years.

Against all odds, enough money was raised to build a new shelter in addition to maintaining 100 animals on average in the barn. In November 2008, the 118 cats who still lived at the barn were moved to their new shelter.

Katie's Place is the pride of the people who run it, and it is beloved by the community which funds it. The animals and their stories have touched people since the shelter opened. They are stories of strength and trust that never died in small, battered hearts. They're stories of becoming the family for some who called the shelter home for life. They're stories of solace for a few who were too buffeted by life and lost their fight. Not all the animals made it to new homes, but each and every one was loved. We hope you enjoy their stories.

A King Among Cats

We had never heard of FIV (Feline Immunodeficiency Virus) or FeLV (Feline Leukemia) until a cat came to us testing positive for both. We understood these viruses were not contagious to any other species but were contagious among cats. This presented a dilemma. We wouldn't turn away a cat in need, and we wouldn't euthanize a cat who could still enjoy life. But this new tom couldn't live in the communal room, nor could any of us foster him since we all had cats at home. Big black Solo lived in a makeshift cage on the hall floor for the first couple of weeks.

He was trapped by another rescuer who had no place for him. One of our volunteers went to get him, coaxing him into a carrier with a pair of thick gloves for protection. Solo was a piece of work! Mean and hissing, he lay in the dark recesses of his cage, and all we could see was the yellow glow of his eyes, narrowed to slits. Only the bravest of us attempted to clean his cage each day.

Our policy since the beginning is that we make no judgment on whose life is worth rescuing. The sick, elderly, and homely are as precious to us as the healthy, young, and attractive. This is the heart of our mandate. However scrappy and sick he might be, Solo had our protection. We built another room across the hall from the Main Pen. It had a window and would be comfortable since it seemed he would be with us for a while – unless someone came along wanting a hostile cat with FIV and Feline Leukemia.

When the room was secure, we took Solo's cage inside and opened it, suggesting to him that he might come out once we were on the other side of the door. Solo crept out of the cage and settled himself into a nest. Even at rest, he seemed like a coiled spring, watchful and ready. We kept one eye on him as we cleaned his room each day. Solo watched us from his roost, making no move and betraying no emotion.

Among our ranks was a volunteer who could match ornery for ornery with any cat. She wouldn't take any guff, and she loved animals with all her heart. She was the one who wrangled Solo to Katie's Place from his rescuer's home. One day Magda was cleaning his pen and felt Solo watching her as usual. Dropping her broom, she muttered, "This is ridiculous, you and I are going to be friends, and that's that." She pulled Solo onto her lap and began stroking him. Solo was caught by surprise and sat frozen for a long, tense moment. Then she felt his muscles relax as he began to move in her lap. She kept her guard up but continued stroking him. He twisted to face her, and a low rumbling rose from his throat. Solo was purring. He looked up at her, his eyes still wary but questioning. His face had softened. Time with dry beds and regular meals had been good for his coat. He looked clean and felt soft. Solo was actually quite a handsome cat.

That was the beginning of a long and special relationship. Solo remained low key and undemonstrative by nature, but he always purred when we stopped to stroke him. He never generated any inquiries from adopters. It's hard to find homes for plain, black, adult males which are healthy. It's even harder when they have FIV and Feline Leukemia. The shelter was Solo's home, and we became his family.

As time passed, other FIV and Feline Leukemia cats came to live in Solo's room. We expanded his room and added an attached porch. They had lots of space. But being adult males, most of whom were not neutered before coming to us, they jockeyed for supremacy sometimes. Quarrels broke out, and the more submissive cats scurried for cover while the aggressors strutted and swaggered. Solo watched these performances with disinterest. He wasn't intimidated by any other cat, and he didn't care to challenge any of them either.

Solo was the leader. He knew it and didn't have to defend it. If an up-and-comer advanced on him, intending to make a point, Solo dispatched him with a swipe. He was powerfully built, and all he wanted was a peaceful life. Once the contender had slunk off to rethink his position in the hierarchy, Solo resumed his meditations unperturbed. The weaker cats learned they could bed down next to Solo and enjoy his protection. Many a cat found comfort at Solo's side, nestled against his flanks. He was calm and gentle with a clearly compassionate side. However much the cats might squirm and fuss beside him, Solo never lost patience with them.

Once the boys were altered, their hormones subsided. They became accustomed to their new home and roommates. Skirmishes were really quite rare, and groups of them became close, sleeping together and becoming family for each other. Solo was never part of any one group. He was trusted by all.

The FIV and Feline Leukemia viruses shorten a cat's life. These cats are as robust as any cat until they begin to wear down. Their health might then falter a few times as they fight off infections. When the end comes, it seems rather rapid. They lose their appetite and fade quickly. We lost several FIV and Feline Leukemia cats over the years. Cats that Solo came to know well succumbed, and toward the end, he could be seen at their sides, licking their heads and lying beside them for a while in silent camaraderie.

By February 2004, Solo had been with us for three years. The vet estimated his age to be about thirteen or fourteen years. He was beginning to have spells of poor health. He got past his rough spells and carried on. But we knew he was living on borrowed time. By mid-December 2004, we were monitoring his health closely. He was not doing well, and it was time to watch for the moment when life ceases to be a blessing and becomes a burden.

Solo reached that moment on Christmas Eve 2004. All the volunteers were notified, and one volunteer came to the shelter after working a graveyard shift so he could spend a few hours with him. They sat together in their favourite position, David stretched out on the couch and Solo curled up on his chest, seemingly lost in a reverie deeper than any before.

Solo left us that day. It was the end of an era when he had ruled as Benevolent Patriarch. Some cats, you never forget. Solo was one.

The Cat Who Chose Her Own Homes

Cairo was living homeless in a ravine. A concerned homeowner captured her and brought her to Katie's Place. She was a long-haired cat with pale tortie points and a vaguely Persian face. The look on her face when she surveyed her new surroundings for the first time was reminiscent of Bette Davis's famous utterance, "What a dump!" Cairo was imperious, self assured and opinionated. To say that she was not pleased to find herself at the shelter would be an understatement. We wondered how her rescuers managed to capture her and keep their hands intact.

Her long coat was badly matted after her sojourn in the ravine. We suspected that it had been her home for some time. She needed to be shaved to the skin, and she returned to the shelter with a lion cut that left her with large furry booties and a large furry head atop a small, bony body. She was an older girl. Underneath fur, age is as unforgiving of cats as it is of people. Skin loses elas-

ticity, and Cairo's undercarriage hung nearly to the
floor between her hind
paws. She had a tremen-
dous sense of dignity and
demanded respect from
everyone. But nothing
could save her from our
amusement at the sight of
her. She gave us her best
withering look and chose
to ignore us.

     Nobody was going to
adopt this irascible little cat. We volunteers saw how
much character she had though, and one of us eventually
took her home.

     Cairo settled into the household and seemed to
thrive in Trish's home. So it was a mystery when she
disappeared one day. Trish was beside herself. She felt
terrible that Cairo managed to escape, and she hated the
thought of the old cat out there somewhere, huddled in
the dark, scared and miserable. She searched and put up
posters. Finally, she canvassed the neighbourhood for
news of the little cat. What she learned surprised us
although it shouldn't have, knowing Cairo. A neighbour
reported that Cairo was living with him. She came and
went, but she was there enough that he came to regard
her as his cat. Trish probed until she was certain they
were talking about the same animal. If this was Cairo's
wish, Trish wouldn't fight it, although she felt a bit
wounded that Cairo wanted to leave.

A week or two passed, and Trish came to the shelter one day with the news that Cairo had returned. She tried to keep her inside now. But in a family with kids, doors are constantly opened, and Cairo was the kind of cat to dedicate herself to getting what she wanted. If escape was her goal, she would escape. Sure enough, one day she disappeared again. This time, the neighbour down the street said he hadn't seen her for a while. Again Trish canvassed the neighbourhood. After talking to several people, she found another neighbour who reported that Cairo had moved in with them.

It seemed that Cairo invited herself into any home that would have her. She was friendly when she wanted to be, and cat lovers were pleased to let her stay. When the spirit moved her, Cairo deserted her latest residence. Perhaps that ravine had been the home of her choice until she was captured. If so, it's no wonder she looked so disgruntled to find herself at the shelter.

The Professor

The Professor had been hanging around a neighbourhood for at least three years. A compassionate neighbour watched for him, but the wily cat always eluded capture until finally he let his guard down. He tested positive for both Feline Immunodeficiency Virus (FIV) and Feline Leukemia, so he joined Solo, who also had the viruses, in his new pen.

The Professor took almost no time to adjust. He sat by the door, mumbling constantly while he watched us moving around. If he caught our eye, his murmurs rose in pitch as he leaned forward, willing us to respond. He had wide-spaced ears, sleepy eyes, and a large muzzle with a set to his mouth that gave him a mournful expression. Despite his lugubrious look, he was a good-natured and trusting cat who accepted us into his life as though he'd been waiting for us. If we went into the Boys' Pen and sat down, he hurried over, muttering excitedly, and hopped into our laps where he drank in as much affection as he could coax from us. When we cleaned in his room, he followed us around, mumbling conversationally.

We posted the Professor on Petfinder.com although we held out little hope of finding a home for a shabby cat with FIV and Feline Leukemia. Against all odds, we had an inquiry one day. A gentleman who lived in downtown Vancouver was intrigued by his story. He might also have been attracted by his name. The man reminded us of a professor himself as we read his e-mails.

The gentleman came out to Maple Ridge to meet our Professor. We invited him to sit down in the Boys' Pen, predicting that in mere seconds, this friendly cat would be in his lap. The Professor was watching from a corner as we talked with the new person in his pen. Then the man sat down. A lap! Ever in lap-seeking mode, the Professor made a beeline across the room to claim his prize before another cat could arrive. That clinched it. He had found his match. They went home together where the Professor delighted his new person, and his new person delighted us with reports on his progress.

"As soon as he arrived, he marched round the place, measuring up and poking in every corner. He let me know it's not quite what he's bred to, but it'll do – for the time being. Right now he's snoozing on my chair. But this is only one of the several spots he's marked out for extensive comfort trials. He's taken several looks at the bathtub, inside and out, and I gave him a full demo of the faucet. He thinks it's pretty cool as a bar facility."

The last e-mail told us the Professor was enjoying everything he'd missed as a long-term street cat. "When I come in after wasting time getting paid (and after I've served dinner and we've passed the port, so to speak), he's teaching me how to play hide and seek by tearing through the apartment from end to end and finding plenty of places to hide."

A couple of years went by and the Professor even got a website when his person learned about creating web pages. Inevitably, the old cat's health began to falter as time passed. His adoption was a permanent foster situation. We retained responsibility for any veterinary expenses incurred. The Professor had a home, the gentleman had an amiable companion, and we had one less cat to look after at the shelter. Win-win. When the Professor needed veterinary care one day, he came back to our vet in Maple Ridge for treatment.

We visited him at the vet's and found him to be as tolerant of the unexpected as when he first arrived at Katie's Place. He sat at the front of his cage, and his face showed just the barest hint of surprise to find himself in this place. When he returned home, the man and cat resumed life together, enjoying each other's company as much as ever. But veterinary treatment only forestalled the inevitable, giving them a few more months.

We got the e-mail in 2004 advising us that the Professor had passed away. Though the message was brief, we read the man's sorrow through the words. This sweet-tempered cat had touched many people in his time. He would be missed.

The Ugly Cat

Ramsey was homely. Even to a cat lover, Ramsey was not pretty. He was stocky and squat in build. He held his ragged, pointed ears slightly flattened in a defensive posture. His eyes were narrowed with the untrusting, defeated look of a convict. The black and white markings on his face slanted up on one side, giving him a permanent sneer. Life on the streets completed his look with a grubby coat, yellowed fur that was once white and a furtive demeanor. Newer volunteers recoiled from this little beast. It took a seasoned volunteer with a soft spot for the hard cases to see anything noble in Ramsey. We put him in a new-cat cage where he made himself invisible under his bedding. He had no use for humans, not after a lifetime of rejection.

We cleaned his cage around him and let him be. The mistrust was mutual. Was this cat feral? Could he be touched or would he slash at hands that reached under his bedding? We didn't know, and we didn't care to experiment. But the seasoned volunteer, Carol, could not resist a challenge. The tougher the case, the more determined she became to find his soft spot. Climbing right into Ramsey's cage, she would sit still and talk softly to the lump under the bedding. She began bringing a toy on a stick which she wiggled at edge of the blanket. One day, a broad, yellowed paw shot out at the toy. She wiggled it again, and the paw batted at it. Ramsey was playing.

Always pushing the boundaries, Carol began to reach her hand under the bedding. We watched as the lump under the blanket moved. It seemed there had been friendly contact. There was no hasty retreat; no blood. Then Carol began rolling the bedding back until a broad, sneering face squinted up at her, flinching as though half expecting abuse. She stroked Ramsey's cheeks and gave him time to assess her. Before long, his squat little body sat beside her in the cage, and he began leaning into her caresses. We started to see Ramsey in a different light. He was still ugly, but there was a vulnerability and innocence about him as he sat at his new friend's knees and enjoyed being stroked. He gazed up at her with eyes that now showed more longing and sadness than distrust or hostility. His lopsided markings showed less of a sneer as the set of his mouth softened.

Among his other problems, Ramsey contracted Feline Leukemia (FeLV) and Feline Immunodeficiency Virus (FIV) during his time on the streets. After a few weeks, he graduated from his new-cat cage to the Boys' Pen with the other FeLV/FIV+ cats. Now he had a whole new challenge. He had accepted these humans as friends, but now he was surrounded by other cats, and experience had taught him that other cats were competitors for food and shelter. The harder it is for strays to meet their needs, the more fiercely they will fight. Ramsey wasn't a fighter at heart. There was no swaggering alpha male in this cat. He revealed himself more and more to be a sensitive, childlike soul who only fought when cornered and who felt intense grief at rejection.

To Ramsey's relief, the few fights in the Boys' Pen were more like siblings' squabbles than battles for survival. Food was plentiful, and since they were altered, the hormones that instigate most battles had subsided. Gradually, Ramsey discovered that he was safe, and he became part of the gang. When we went into the Boys' Pen to sit, Ramsey joined the other cats in competing for lap space. This competition was harmless jostling and not like the savage warfare of the streets.

Love and care restored Ramsey's physical condition until he became a handsome fellow. His coat grew clean and plush. His white fur was snowy. He held his ears high and proud. Clear, green eyes met our gaze with trust and affection. Ramsey became a much-beloved member of our family, and he returned our affection in full measure. He had endured hardship for most of his life. Now, distant memories of kittenhood in a home resurfaced, and Ramsey took to life at the shelter with joy. As homes go, it was humble. But he was safe and loved, and he was happy.

The legacy of life on the streets – the FIV and Feline Leukemia – meant Ramsey's time would not be long. He had arrived in January 2002. By the end of the summer in 2003, his health was failing. He lost weight and his fur grew dull. We knew we would soon have to help him pass. We spent as much time with him as possible in the last couple of days. He began to withdraw into himself when his body started to fail. He finally stopped greeting us at the door, and we missed the grateful eagerness that had so endeared him to us. On September 3, 2003, we let him go. We comforted ourselves that he was happy in his last months. Our ugly little boy had become beautiful.

The Cat Who Didn't Want a Home

Taz's story starts before Katie's Place began. She was brought to the municipal shelter because of illness in her family. A volunteer who would one day work for Katie's Place was there when Taz arrived, and she watched the elegant, gray-and-white cat that the woman held with one arm while signing the release papers with the other. Taz seemed calm and only a bit curious about this place.

They put her in a cage in the small-animal room where she looked around in bewilderment. If she hadn't felt that anything was wrong before, she did now. She allowed her cage to be cleaned but smacked any hands that attempted to pick her up. The last human touch she had tolerated was her own person's. Days passed as Taz waited for her person to return. She became harder to handle as her grief turned to anger. One day she darted out of her cage during cleaning. The volunteer was working in the yard behind the buildings when staff retrieved the angry little cat using a catchpole with a noose. She could hear Taz's screams through closed doors as they dragged her back to her cage by her neck.

The municipal shelter volunteers took Taz to a couple of adoptathons they organized at local malls. She was well behaved but couldn't be petted. She needed time to restore her trust. They found a foster home for her and hoped the situation might become a permanent adoption. After several weeks, the people returned her. She had remained aloof, and they could no longer keep her. Taz had run out of options.

That would have been the end for her in an oft-repeated cycle at similar facilities. Some unwanted pets take loss harder than others, and their last days or weeks are spent in fear, confusion and loneliness – a wretched way to end life. But by this time, a few volunteers had set up a room in a barn and were taking a few desperate cats. Taz went to live there, becoming one of the first residents of what would be Katie's Place. Released into the communal room, she leapt to a high perch, defying anyone to approach her. She took no interest in the volunteers, but she seemed content in her new accommodations. She didn't mind the other cats if they stayed out of her way, and there was room enough for them to avoid each other.

Several more cats came to the barn over the next months, and several were adopted. The incoming animals always seemed to exceed the outgoing by a slight margin so that the population grew. Taz was nonchalant about the growth of Katie's Place. It was gradual enough that she adjusted easily. She was a bright, observant little cat who sized up newcomers, two-legged and four-legged, and let them know where they stood with her. Leave me alone and we'll get along fine was her rule. Those who broke that rule were reminded of it with extended claws and an outraged squawk. She was a tiny cat but she commanded respect. Everyone gave her space and she lived her life serenely in her own world.

Months turned to years, and adopters never inquired about her. We had to be honest in our description on the web and referred to her as feisty and spirited – words that didn't fool anyone. Visitors who showed interest in the dapper little cat were soon discouraged by Taz who rejected friendly gestures without preamble. She swiped at encroaching fingers and retreated out of reach. During the bustle of open hours, she found a perch away from the crowd and slumbered, ignoring the activity behind her.

Taz was happy. She never knew a day of ill health. She could sometimes be seen wriggling playfully in a nest, absorbed in a game where she was the only player. In the quiet hours of early morning when a volunteer arrived to feed and clean before going to work, Taz responded to her name being called and came to spend a few moments with the volunteer. But she never allowed herself to be picked up and only tolerated caresses for a few seconds.

Of all the house cats who came to the shelter over the years, Taz is one we never promoted for adoption. We let her be. Katie's Place is her home. She's lived there for nine years as of this writing. She's starting to show her age which must be approaching fifteen years. Her fur is less glossy, and her body has grown angular. But she's still agile and graceful, confident and content.

Taz turned her back on the human species when she lost the one human she ever loved. She gave her whole heart to that first person and never gave it away again. Her life belongs solely to herself now, and she lives it on her own terms among her 'staff' who obediently feed her, and the feline rabble who obediently avoid her.

On the Pleasures of Best Friends and TV, and Shrinking Violets

During the first year, Katie's Place accepted several cats from a trailer park where they had multiplied from a few abandoned pets to a small, ragged colony. Three of these were tabby-and-white siblings we called Shady, Sherlock and Violet. They were a year old when they arrived at the shelter, too old to socialize. We let them loose in the Main Pen where they promptly dashed off in different directions and hid. A later search revealed Violet's face peering nervously at us from behind a chair. Shady's eyes glowed from the depths of a hidey hole, and Sherlock's face glowered from the rafters at the top of the porch.

The siblings weren't completely feral. They had been fed by neighbours and had learned to associate humans with kindness. A volunteer resolutely tried to win Violet's trust, sitting with the youngster held firmly in her lap while stroking her. Violet seemed to enjoy the caresses in spite of herself. She looked up with tender

Violet

vulnerability in her face that could break your heart. She was a tiny cat and a timid one. But she was the first to accept us. Her brother Shady was more robust and was more skeptical of our intentions. He watched us from a high nest with detached interest as we cajoled him to come and play with a toy we offered. Sherlock was the holdout. He made himself invisible, spending his time in the recesses of the rafters while we were around. If we climbed up to peek at him, he shrank back and crept away to hide.

They lived in the Main Pen for a year and a half, adjusting to shelter life and making friends among the other cats. They accepted our presence, acknowledging us as part of their world, but never seeking human company. They really had no chance of getting out of the shelter. Adopters weren't interested in cats who didn't want to be petted. As healthy three-year-olds, they faced a long life within the shelter walls unless someone gave them a chance. They inhabited an in-between world where they depended on humans while never learning to trust them.

In autumn of 2003, one of our volunteers decided to adopt Shady and Violet.

Shady

These two tolerated our attention quite well. Sherlock, however, still refused all contact with us and was a name without a face for many of the volunteers. He was happy with his feline friends. The adoption was an act of compassion on Kathy's part. Shady and Violet accepted us but did not welcome us with purrs and leg rubs as other cats would. Kathy offered them a home without expecting anything from them. As it turned out, they would surprise her.

Shady and Violet took time to adjust. That was expected. They hid under beds or under the couch for a long time, coming out to eat and play when the house was quiet. At least they were eating. Gradually they began to recognize Kathy and her husband. Human presence at the shelter was variable and sporadic compared to home life with one family. Violet began by bonding strongly with Kathy's cat, Louis. Where Louis lay down, Violet lay with him. Then Violet began seeking human company. Now it didn't take long before Violet appeared as soon as anyone sat on the couch, kneading her paws in their lap and "purring like mad." Shady also flourished with home life, but what distinguished him was his fascination with the TV. Kathy said he probably watched an hour or two a day.

As for Sherlock, he developed an especially deep bond with another semi-feral youngster who arrived a couple of months after he had. Arizona was one of a family of six cats trapped at four months of age, and he had little contact with humans before coming to the shelter. Sherlock and Arizona became inseparable. They slept together, groomed each other and moved as one.

The whole time they lived at the shelter, their devotion never wavered. We often saw them watching us from high nests, cheek to cheek.

We noticed Sherlock with a wound on his head one day, probably sustained in a squabble. We captured him and put him in a single-cat enclosure so we could treat the wound and ensure it didn't become infected. Sherlock was as forlorn in confinement as a vigorous young cat could be. A few days into his treatment, he saw his chance to make a break. A volunteer was cleaning his enclosure. Sherlock was curled up at the back one minute, and the next minute, he darted between her arms and catapulted himself to a high perch where stopped and looked back at her, almost seeming to laugh. Knowing he was out of reach, he ambled along a shelf, hopped across a gap, and met Arizona trotting toward him. The two settled together on the highest perch and exchanged heartfelt nuzzles of greeting. Their happiness was so apparent that we didn't try to isolate Sherlock again. The wound was healing well. We could monitor it from a distance.

Robust young cats like Sherlock and Arizona should not live out their lives within shelter walls. One of the volunteers owned property outside of town and set up a feral colony on her land. Katie's Place had special fencing erected to enclose a piece of the property which included woods, cleared land and a little cabin that was converted into a shelter. In 2007, Sherlock and Arizona were among a number of ferals who were rounded up and taken to the property. There they would enjoy freedom to run and sunbathe without human intrusion. The volunteer monitors the colony. She puts food out, cleans the cabin and manages to keep tabs on the cats as they roam the meadow and melt into the undergrowth. One tree in particular has become a favourite nest. Looking up, she can always see eyes peering down at her from the branches. Sherlock is easy to spot with his distinctive tabby-and-white markings. Arizona is harder to distinguish being pure black among other black cats. But it's a safe bet that the black cat at Sherlock's side is his best friend, Arizona.

Arizona and Sherlock

The Tiny Tyrant

A Katie's Place volunteer was walking past a park one day when she spied a lump at the side of the road that looked odd. Something about it awoke all her instincts. Fixing her gaze on it, she drew closer and saw that it was a rabbit. She hoped it would dart into a burrow. Katie's Place was full and the volunteers were not looking for new animals. But the rabbit remained motionless even when she stood over it. It won't let me pick it up, she told herself, it'll scoot off. She bent over the huddled creature and gathered it into her arms. It won't stay still for long, she thought, it'll struggle to escape and then run to its burrow. But the little rabbit rested in her arms, seeming to relax. She had no choice now. She put the rabbit in a spare carrier she kept in her car, and off they went to Katie's Place.

The volunteers who were cleaning looked up with trepidation when she approached with a carrier in hand. What now? They watched as she opened it on the counter in the office, and when the rabbit's head popped up, they broke into smiles of delight in spite of themselves.

The bunny was a Netherland Dwarf, an adorable morsel of pale gray fur with small round ears and big round eyes. Carol lifted it out and set it on the counter. It was a female, and she sat up tall, looking around with alert curiosity. She had perked up considerably from the frightened bunny that crouched motionless in the grass. They set up a cage in the corner of the office-kitchen area, and they named her Allie McBinky.

Bunnies are often turned loose in parks when they become inconvenient to their families. People assume they can eat grass and fend for themselves. Such 'freedom' is usually fatal for pet rabbits. But they do have time to reproduce, starting a stream of unwanted rabbits to die prematurely. Allie was lucky to be rescued. Her new-admission vet check revealed that she was an older bunny and had misaligned teeth which needed regular trimming. Allie might have been abandoned because of her age and her teeth. She was a high-maintenance pet. As we got to know her, we began to see another reason for someone to abandon her. Allie turned out to be a cantankerous little soul. We joked that somebody probably turned her loose thinking God help the coyote or dog that tangles with her.

The first rule Allie set was Don't Mess with My Stuff. Her cage was her turf, and when the volunteers tried to clean it, she became agitated and rushed at their hands grunting fiercely. Cleaning the cage was a battle involving cautious advances and hasty retreats. In the end, it was best to remove Allie and let her roam the front office until her cage was finished. Allie enjoyed these excursions and ambled around, peering into every corner. She squeezed under shelves and emerged farther down with cobwebs trailing from her fur.

Often we left her out to enjoy her free time for a while with the doors closed. A new problem arose with that. Allie expanded her territory to include the office-kitchen area, and she defended it as vigorously as she defended her cage. If anyone came in, the tiny rabbit charged them from whichever corner she'd been exploring, uttering her singular battle cries. The sight of a frenzied rabbit rushing at them from out of nowhere and grunting wildly caused people to back up in alarm. It didn't matter that she was tiny. She was a menacing presence. Allie's sense of power increased each time she managed to rout a trespasser from her office. Returning her to the cage became a military manoeuver, undertaken only by experienced volunteers who planned their approach before going in.

Volunteers who wrangled semi-feral cats and popped pills down their throats were not put off by a tyrannical bunny. When it was time to clip Allie's growing teeth, they grabbed her quickly and confidently, secured her in their laps and commenced clipping. Sensing she was outranked, Allie became docile, and they completed the procedure with relative ease. It was an impressive thing to witness. The volunteer who clipped leaned in to gauge the cut as another volunteer held Allie firmly in position. A snap resounded as the teeth gave way under the clipper. Allie never struggled. She recognized when she was outnumbered and outflanked.

Once she knew she couldn't intimidate you, she became meek and enjoyed a cuddle. She stretched out in one volunteer's lap with her hind legs extended, her large feet bottom side up at his knees. We were keen to find her a home, as much because she enjoyed human company as because we wanted our office back. One day people came to meet her who wanted a friend for their bunny at home. We told them about Allie as they experienced her personality first hand. We hold nothing back from adopters since it does no good for the animal nor the adopters to end up parting ways over unrevealed details. They decided they could work with her and they drove off with her carrier on the seat between them.

The next day, a car rolled into the parking lot at a good clip, and we heard the door open and close with businesslike emphasis. One of Allie's adopters came in with Allie McBinky held gingerly in outstretched arms. Handing her to the first volunteer he met, he explained that Allie would not work out in their home. She had beaten up their rabbit. If she had made herself unpleasant in other ways, he didn't linger to elaborate. Casting a last leery look at her, he turned and left. Allie perched in the crook of the volunteer's elbow with casual jauntiness as though she had expected to be back. Apparently this nasty little bunny with the adorable Disney-character face was going to be hard to place.

She resumed her reign in the office. Several weeks later, another couple came to meet her who already had a rabbit, guinea pigs and a dog at home. They were experienced animal people who, when told about the legendary Allie McBinky, felt up to the challenge of living with her. They took her home, and we waited nervously for

the sound of tires skid-
ding over gravel that
would announce Allie's
return. The sound never
came.

   By Christmastime,
we were planning our
biggest fund raiser of the
year, Pet Photos with
Santa, and we had put
Allie out of our minds.
Several of our alumni
return each year for their
own photos with Santa. Their new families are as proud
to show them off as we are happy to see them. By early
afternoon, we had ushered out the umpteenth subject,
and the next one appeared. It was ridiculously tiny compared to the large dogs we'd been posing at Santa's
knees. Allie McBinky had returned, not to stay, but for a
photo with Santa.

   Her new family regaled us with Allie stories as we
positioned the little rabbit in Santa's arms. Her bunny
friend was tolerant enough to be a good match for her.
She liked to gather as much hay in her mouth as she
could and throw it at him. He sat stoically, covered in
hay, never seeming to mind. The family's Rottweiler,
however, learned to slink away in fear at the sight of her.
They enjoyed her feistiness and had no trouble handling
her. They thought she was hilarious. We did too as we
perched a miniature Santa hat on her head for the photo.
It was an indignity we couldn't resist. She didn't move,

she merely glared mutinously as we took her photo. If looks could kill.... Her retribution, once they were all home again, was something her family could deal with.

Allie continued to keep things lively in her house until her death at a good old age, more than three years later. Her family still speaks of her with amusement and affection.

Seven Destinies for Seven Siblings

In early summer 2002, a family of kittens was born in a train yard at Boston Bar. Workers saw them playing in the grass around the yard. They feared what would happen to the youngsters in the cold Boston Bar winter, so they trapped them and brought them to Katie's Place. We put the terrified little family into one of our cat condos (our larger version of a cage) where they huddled together with tense faces.

They were a handsome group. Oscar was a long-haired tabby with a rusty orange coat. Elmo was black with a white undercarriage and paws. Dixie was a long-haired torbie, as vibrantly coloured as Oscar. Zeke was gray and white, and Alfie was black with white paws and bib. Sharla and Clarence were black and white, Clarence with a stocky build; Sharla, daintier.

They were about four months old and had never been handled by humans. Whether they became affectionate house pets or developed a permanent fear of humans depended on their personality and how much socializing they received during this critical period in their youth.

Oscar was adopted right away by one of the workers who rescued him. He would socialize well in their home with their other cat setting a companionable example. The others went into foster care where they could get more human contact than we could give them at the shelter. The youngsters bonded immediately with older cats in the home, following them adoringly. Cats had always been their social world, and an adult cat was their first choice of mentor. The older cats accepted this hero worship with bemusement or indifference.

Their foster parents soon began seeing strong differences in each kitten's personality. Elmo was a bold, confident clown, enthusiastic to try anything new. He was the first to explore their foster home. He soon included the human family in his circle of friends, sleeping on the bed at night and enjoying cuddles. When the youngsters returned to the shelter, Elmo was adopted within a few weeks by a teacher who sometimes took him to school. Being a gregarious cat by nature, he tolerated this well and seemed as entertained by the children as they were by him.

Elmo

The other youngsters reserved judgment about humans. When their foster mom wasn't coaxing them to accept her touch without cringing, they spent their time within their own little pack. They played with anything they could find. Dried flower arrangements were a particular favourite because of the satisfying crunch they made when pounced upon. Foster Mom checked on unusual noises and would find a flower arrangement reduced to a bunch of broken stems, or books pulled off the shelves and bearing tiny teeth marks on the corners. The room appeared deserted, the culprits taking cover at the sound of human feet. If she stood long enough, eyes peeped out inquiringly from under various pieces of furniture. But the games did not resume until she left.

The kittens went through a bout of cat flu with stuffed noses and weepy eyes. Any cat who endures the stress of coming into shelter care is exposed once they're among other cats. It's a common ailment from which most recover in a couple of weeks with antibiotics to fight opportunistic bugs that can take hold while they're weakened. Alfie was small and fragile, and he was hit hard by the flu. He was fine-boned with a plume of a tail that he held proudly aloft. He had grown comfortable in the same room with humans although he never completely lost the wariness he learned at birth. If anyone came too close, he scampered away and turned to watch them cheekily once he was out of reach. The cat flu took the zip right out of him. For quite a while, he was listless and showed no interest in food or games. Cats are unique in that going without food for a long period can be fatal.

Alfie's foster mom knew he was in a bad way when she was able to pick him up. He lay dull-eyed in her arms, and she felt a chill in the pit of her stomach. Day after day, she cradled him with his head in the crook of her elbow as she spoon-fed him. He accepted the food and allowed her to wipe his runny nose and eyes. Her heart went out to the tiny cat. Gradually he became stronger until he was healthy enough to scoot away from her again. He enjoyed his food but insisted on eating from a plate on the floor. She was both relieved and disappointed when he was fit enough to evade her and forget the cuddling they'd enjoyed. Because he was fragile, and because he'd stolen her heart, he stayed with her when the others returned to the shelter.

Dixie

The youngster who tolerated humans the least was Dixie. Though she did most of her growing up among humans, she remained a wild spirit who grew saucer-eyed at the sight of humans and shrank into the shadows to avoid them. She made her home with another volunteer where she showed progress over time.

Once she realized her new human was not stalking her, they could occupy the same room. She attached herself to an older cat in that household and cried in distress if he slipped away while she was napping. Her worst nightmare was when he was in a human lap. He was out of her reach, and not even her need for him pulled her past the invisible six-foot barrier she had erected. A year later, she allowed her person as close as six inches, but she still wouldn't allow contact.

Zeke, Sharla and Clarence returned to the shelter. They still did not fully accept humans, but they were confident around them and needed to become accustomed to different people. Zeke grew excep-

Zeke

tionally handsome. His fur was a glorious mane around a well-proportioned face with dark copper eyes. He was a charmer who enjoyed our company more and more until a visitor fell under his spell and adopted him.

Clarence

Clarence was at the other extreme, glaring resentfully every time we invaded his space. A tough little bounder, he played vigorous games with his feline friends and liked wrestling them to the ground. But he stayed as far from humans as he could get. Eventually, he went to a feral colony with a number of his feral pals.

Sharla stayed with us the longest and bonded deeply with different cats over the years. Her first friend was a ginger tabby with a bad heart. Guinness couldn't exert himself to move much, and Sharla spent many hours at his side. After he passed away, she took up with a phleg-matic black-and-white cat named Pancake. They passed the afternoons lying by the window, watching the other cats and nuzzling each other. If people approached,

Sharla moved to another perch and discouraged any further interest with a withering glance.

Oscar (top) and Sharla

Two years later, she was adopted by the same people who brought her family down from Boston Bar and who kept her brother, Oscar. She didn't remember Oscar, but they accepted each other with the semi-feral's preference for feline company that was still strong in them. The surprise was how well she accepted her humans. Within four months, she greeted them at the door and slept on the bed with them.

"Mornings are fun," her person wrote, "she head-rubs me until I'm awake with a mouth full of fur. She likes to be patted. Her front end goes down, and up comes the rear as if on hydraulics. She starts purring, then she rolls to the side or walks three steps, and we start again. This goes on through the full length of the hall or until our knees give out."

As for Alfie, he eventually allowed his people to stroke him, and he slept on the bed with them. He loved their other cats, particularly a large tabby named Tomorrow. Then, in January 2005, he became unusually quiet. This little imp never stayed still for long, so it aroused concern. His person took him to the vet's, and they discovered that he had intestinal cancer.

She wrote, "It came so quickly! Just at Christmas, he was enjoying a new game. I'd put a Christmas table-cloth over the coffee table and it touched the floor. He discovered he could hide under it and jump out at passers by with quite a delightful reaction. (He didn't realize his tail was sticking out. He gave a surprised chirp when we touched it.) After the bad news on Wednesday, I looked at him on Friday and realized it was time. A week before, he had seemed his usual self! I took him to the vet in his favourite basket with his red tartan blanket. He lay quietly and gave a squeaky little meow a couple of times, only a shadow of his normal squeaky meow. I touched him and talked to him during the trip."

Alfie was helped to pass, still wrapped in his red tartan blanket. His person remained at his side until the end. He took a part of her heart with him. She always presented a stoic face to the world, but there was no mistaking that he had been special to her, and she to him.

Alfie

Nickleby's Eyes

Animals, like people, differ in their sensitivity.
Some are tough as nails, hardy and unshakeable. Arriving at a shelter is an adventure for them. Others are
timid, sensitive creatures for whom upheaval is agonizing. Nickleby was the latter type.

He came to us when his people moved away and left
him behind. How bonded he had been with his people,
how hurtful it was to lose them, we'll never know. But
we can be certain that finding himself alone and locked
out of his old home was bewildering and, for a cat like
Nickleby, utterly terrifying. Everything familiar disappeared except the building itself and any rubbish. He
would have prowled anxiously around and around the
perimeter, trying to find a way in, unable to comprehend
that this was no longer his home.

Another family saw the neighbour's black cat still
hanging around the house, and they felt for him. His pain
must have been as obvious to them as it was to us when
we met him. They put food out which he ate despite his
nervousness. But they were unable to give him a home

and they brought him to Katie's Place. Like many new cats, he was uneasy and tried to make himself invisible in a corner of his new-cat cage. Something about his eyes set him apart though. Many cats are distressed for a long time after arriving at the shelter. But none ever had eyes as full of pathos as Nickleby's. For the first few days, he huddled motionless in his cage with downcast eyes. When he finally summoned the courage to look us in the face, his eyes were wide and brimming with profound hurt. They were questioning, as if he wondered what had gone wrong. They were vulnerable and as guileless as a child. Those eyes never held a moment of anger. All they showed was pure grief. It never occurred to him to lash out. If he felt overwhelmed, he simply hid.

The time came to release him into a communal room. It was easy to forget about him since he did his best to avoid both humans and other cats. Every so often, we tracked him down to check on him. We might lift the corner of a blanket draped over a chair and find Nickleby crouched underneath. Then he would turn those eyes on us and cause our breath to catch at the sight of such raw sadness.

Time heals when there's time enough, and Nickleby began to recover. We saw him out and about in the communal room; he seemed to be putting the past behind him. His eyes lost their haunted look, and his face took on the calm, inscrutable expression of a normal cat. Soon we would see the side of him that made him so vulnerable. He turned out to be a very loving soul.

Most cats are affectionate with the right people under the right circumstances. It's a myth that they're aloof by nature. But some embrace a relationship with people more than others. Nickleby began waiting for us to visit, and his face brightened as soon as he saw us. He didn't run over to us with the other cats who greeted us. He was too bashful for that. But if we went to where he waited and put a hand out to stroke him, his head reached into the caress; his face beamed with pleasure. Cats can smile, and Nickleby's face smiled with unabashed delight.

He eventually found a new home. He was a plain, black, adult male, the hardest kind of cat to adopt out. But somebody was touched by the ingenuous soul in this cat and wanted him. We'll always remember Nickleby's hurt eyes and the satisfaction it gave us to see them glow with happiness when he finally understood that we loved him.

Heroic Hannah

In January 2003, we took in a cat who seemed little more than a raggedy heap of matted fur. She was a long-haired, tabby-and-white cat who was so matted that she could barely step over the rim of a litter pan. An elderly cat, she was as light and fragile as a bird. She had large, exotically-beautiful eyes. But in those early days at the shelter, they were clouded with bitterness and distrust. Hannah had come from a hard life.

She huddled in her bed in a new-cat condo for a long time after arriving. She seemed angry but resigned as if she'd given up on human kindness. We managed to trim her matted fur away although that ordeal didn't endear us to her. It took several visits to her cage, stroking her gently, to persuade her to raise her head and begin to trust us. In time, she welcomed our visits and enjoyed being petted.

She had the reserved dignity of an old cat. She moved slowly and deliberately, if she moved at all, and she liked to spend her time meditating in her nest. The anger left her eyes and she regarded the world now with the stern expression of a wise, old owl. We could pull her onto our laps where she sat on her backside, her hind legs extended with an abandon that seemed out of character for a self-contained doyenne. She relaxed in this position, yielding to us and evidently enjoying the cuddle despite the disapproving look in her eyes. Disapproval was a natural expression for Hannah's face. Her eyes didn't exactly sparkle with mirth. The closest she came to merriment was to brush past our legs with her back arched and her tail straight up. She never uttered a sound.

Hannah lived in a communal room for many months where she managed to avoid the more active, younger cats. She took no interest in her roommates, nor they in her. Adopters weren't interested in her either. Hannah lived serenely in her own world. In November, we learned she was in the early stages of kidney failure. Age was catching up with her. We could manage her health with a low-protein diet. Since she couldn't eat what the other cats ate and showed no inclination to wander off, we let her live in the common areas of the barn, outside of the communal rooms.

We set up a nest with a thick piece of foam to cushion her old bones, and we left her bowls and litter pan handy for her. Hannah was pleased with this arrangement. Eventually, the piece of foam became grubby, and we replaced it with clean, thick bedding. In fact, we redesigned her corner to give her more space and comfort. We thought she'd enjoy a clean, new corner but she did not. Hannah was upset in her own undemonstrative way. She boycotted the new bed, pointedly sleeping in

inconvenient places with a resentful scowl on her face. We took the hint and retrieved the battered piece of foam, restoring her bed and belongings the way they had been. As soon as that was done, Hannah returned to her corner. She settled into her old bed and her face lightened with an expression approximating happiness. We never messed with her corner again. However, she did allow us to change the towel that covered her foam.

Hannah became affectionate, but she was always restrained, almost dour, in temperament. We never knew her real feelings for us, nor what she was capable of, until an exceptional incident occurred one day.

New cats are segregated until they've acclimatized and have been checked by the vet. This also gives us a chance to see what they're like. Many need time to get over the trauma that brought them into shelter care, and we approach them cautiously until we know them. A senior volunteer was cleaning a new cat's condo one day. He'd been with us for a while and was cranky but not combative. Satisfied that he would stay in his corner, Trish focused on her work. Her head was bent over his litter pan when he was suddenly upon her.

His paw spun like a windmill as he scratched her
arm, and her hand flew up defensively. Darting toward it,
he sank his teeth into the hand that seemed raised in
attack. She snatched her hand back but he hung on. She
was alone in the shelter and barely managed to stay calm,
thinking she wouldn't be able to shake him off and close
the condo door. The thought barely had time to form in
her mind when a shape appeared at her elbow. Hearing
the commotion from her nest, Hannah had dashed across
the room to Trish's side and she lunged at the agitated
cat.

Hannah's appearance caught the cat by surprise, and
he forgot about Trish as he recoiled from Hannah's fury,
backing into a corner of the condo. Trish took the opportunity to yank the condo door closed. Hannah had
jumped down once the cat pulled back, and now she sat
on the floor, barely ruffled, as she seemed to contemplate
what just happened. Trish went to the First Aid kit and
took care of her scratches. When she came back upstairs,
she could see Hannah curled up in her nest at the top of
the stairs.

That corner allowed Hannah the best view of the
whole shelter and allowed volunteers to run their fingers
over her soft head when they passed by. Hannah enjoyed
that as much as they did, and a bond had grown imperceptibly. Now Trish bent over the old cat and stroked her
with new appreciation and a new understanding of how
much devotion Hannah felt in return.

All the volunteers had a new respect for Hannah
after that. She had spirit. But she was aging and not in
the best of health. She never had been very healthy. A

while back, she was adopted briefly and returned when the adopters decided they couldn't deal with her health issues. We didn't list her for adoption again. She was our cat and her home was with us. She followed us around the upstairs as we cleaned, but she never ventured downstairs. She was content with her small realm. We enjoyed her company for another six months after her heroics in November 2003. Then in late May, she collapsed with a stroke.

We rushed her to the vet, and when she came back she seemed to be the same old Hannah. Yet we began seeing signs of fear and confusion that we'd never seen before. The stroke had caused some brain damage. Hannah's comfortable world became an uncertain, frightening place. Her damaged brain would never heal, and it wasn't fair to let her live that way. She'd been through enough. On June 4, 2004, we took her to the vet and let her go. She had been a small, elderly scrap of fur with the heart of a lion, our Hannah.

An Ordinary Cat

Figaro was as plain a creature as ever lived. He was black and white, the most common colour combination among cats. A tuxedo cat with white paws and undercarriage and a white stripe down his nose, he had the most common kind of markings. As a homeless stray, he had the grubby, rangy look of uncared-for cats. He was angular with big feet and a blunt face. He came to us in May 2003 with Feline Immunodeficiency Virus (FIV), no doubt contracted when scrapping with another cat over food or turf.

He lay in his nest, showing neither fear nor friendliness. He didn't seem to have much personality. By now we had forty-five other cats to care for, and when we released Figaro into the Boys' Pen, he blended into the background. The unassuming little cat didn't seek our attention and we didn't seek him out. We saw him sunning on the porch or just sitting, his long body hunched over, forepaws between hind paws in an awkward squat. He was an ungainly fellow. Since he seemed content, we let him be and focused on cats who either needed our attention or demanded it.

Summer ended and Figaro took to spending more time inside. Now we saw more of him and developed more of a relationship with him. He enjoyed attention, and a shy smile seemed to cross his face when he leaned his large, square head into a cheek rub. He had an air of humility as if he himself realized he wasn't the most appealing cat. He was grateful for a bit of affection. When we went into his communal room, we saw him straighten where he sat, as though anticipating, hoping, that we might come over to see him. Figaro seemed to feel honoured when he was singled out. Not being a pretty cat, he would have grown accustomed to being ignored soon after he grew out of the cuteness of kittenhood.

We warmed to this bashful, awkward cat, and he must have sensed our growing warmth toward him. His personality began to blossom. He could be downright comical in the way he flirted, inviting more attention. He rolled over in his nest until all four scrawny legs pointed straight up in the air, and he'd wriggle and twist in his own loose-jointed version of cuteness. It worked. We were enchanted. And he was delighted with our reaction.

It was hard not to love Figaro once you got to know him. We looked forward to a long relationship. But his health began to fail a mere five months after he arrived. He likely caught FIV when he was still quite young. The majority of his life was probably lived on the streets. He was well socialized, so he spent his kittenhood in a human home being cuddled and cooed over. But love must have left his life soon after that. He wasn't an old cat.

We lost Figaro in early October 2003. He declined suddenly, and we saw that he'd reached the end of his road. We had known him such a short time. We barely knew him at all. The image of his ordinary-looking face shining with pleasure when we singled him out for attention will never leave us. If only we could have loved him longer.

An Indomitable Old Cat

Shamus arrived in March 2003. He was a long-term, unaltered street cat and a scrapper. Neighbours fed him, but they tired of his tomcat ways and banded together to trap him. When they brought him to the shelter, he was none too impressed with this turn of events. He sat in his bed, unafraid, and watched us with a skeptical expression. It seemed as though he was waiting for our next move in order to plan his own, like a game of chess.

We let him out of his new-cat cage once he'd been altered and checked by our vet. He reconnoitered the communal room and, having determined its boundaries and that there was no exit, he settled down philosophically. He was as independent a cat as we'd ever met. He didn't particularly care to make friends with us, and he had no use for the other cats. If any of them wandered too close, he swiped at them with a snarl. They skittered away with nervous looks and left him alone. He wasn't a large cat, but he had the air of a commander.

A few months later, Shamus was adopted by someone who had small dogs. He was a handsome Siamese, and we had expected him to find a home. But it didn't last. He considered her dogs amusing at best, annoying at worst, and he toyed with them in his own inimitable way. The woman would not stand to see her dogs terrorized and returned him. Unrepentant, he carried on with life at the shelter.

After a while, we noticed he was losing weight. He'd always been the first to eat, having made his seniority clear to the other cats. But he lost his robust build rapidly, and we took him to the vet for a checkup. He had developed a deep, chronic gingivitis. We didn't know it then, but this was the beginning of a long battle with Shamus's health issues. We tried several medications. However, the gingivitis was impossible to eradicate. In desperation, the vet removed several teeth. Meanwhile, Shamus was not getting enough food in the Main Pen among the hungry hoard. He could never eat enough in one sitting. We decided to let him live in the common areas of the barn where a plate could be available to him until he finished with it.

Moving into the common areas caused a surprising change in Shamus. Aside from gaining some weight, he became a livelier, happier cat. He yelped in pain sometimes when he ate, a sound that made our hearts ache. The gingivitis flared and abated with discouraging regularity, no matter what treatments we tried. Then we heard that St. Paul's Hospital had a specially formulated mouthwash which showed impressive results in human patients with acute stomatitis. They kindly faxed us the recipe and we gave it to our vet. He formulated a cat version; Shamus was the test case. It didn't help. Still, he was a cheerful old bounder who embraced life with enthusiasm.

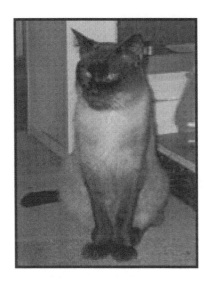

At one point we had to confine him in the Main Pen again because he'd taken to persecuting Katie, the original occupant of the barn and the cat for whom the shelter was named. Katie was a curmudgeon herself and demanded respect. But Shamus was not intimidated. He ran her off for the entertainment of seeing how long it took to make her turn tail and run. We couldn't allow that. The barn belonged to Katie. Shamus seemed to understand that his grounds privileges depended on his good behaviour so, when we released him from the Main Pen, he left Katie alone.

For a while, he lived in a foster home where they could medicate him more frequently. He may have laid down the law with his foster mom and declined treatment because he grew worse, and we brought him back to the shelter. We trialed him on homeopathic remedies. Nothing helped for long. However, he still enjoyed life between the occasional bout of pain when eating. Sometimes when we cleaned the condos, Shamus leapt up beside us. His sudden appearance startled both us and the condo occupant. That was probably his intention. He had a wicked sense of humour.

He was already seven or eight years old when he first came to us, and over time, he grew less active. In the winter of 2006, he voluntarily relinquished Barn Cat status, moving into the Main Pen and almost hibernating until the weather warmed up in spring. By late 2007, he had become frail. He spent most of his time lying in different beds, a skinny cat with cottony, old-cat fur. He responded flirtatiously when we petted him. But he showed little interest in roaming around as he once had. He went into foster care with our volunteer in charge of animal health, Evelyn. She could monitor and medicate him better at home.

He was still chipper despite failing health. He wandered around his foster home with an awkward gait, a cross between an energetic stride and a geriatric stagger, still holding other cats at bay with his belligerent nature. Then as the year turned, he went downhill. On January 2, 2008, the vet came to the house and helped him pass. Evelyn and Magda, volunteers he'd known since he first came to the shelter, were with him that day. We'd like to think their company was good for him, but with Shamus it was always hard to tell. He lay peacefully in a basket and didn't stir when they touched him. There, he drew his last breath. Shamus had lived life on his own terms, independent and fearless to the last.

Like Night and Day

Staff at another shelter admitted a scruffy, black cat in the autumn of 2004. They assessed him over a few days and determined that he was feral. He recoiled from human contact and showed no sign of settling or tolerating a human touch. Cleaning his cage required caution. He was so wild that nobody wanted to try getting him out of his cage into a carrier when he was signed over to Katie's Place. Somehow, it was done. We set him up in a new-cat cage and named him Black Jack. He lay motionless inside his cubby hole for a long time and gave us no reason to expect any improvement. But we stubbornly tried to approach him each time we cleaned his cage.

Some volunteers with soft hearts just can't face reality sometimes and give up. The poor cat's face pulled at their heartstrings. He looked so depressed and lonely. Each day, they reached into his cubby hole to touch him. Eventually, one volunteer got some purrs out of him. Another got him to roll onto his back. It seemed that he was grateful for the attention. Still, he didn't want to leave the safety of his cubby hole. Even the volunteers who refused to give up wondered if he'd come as far as he ever would. This might be another shy cat who slinks into dark corners and stays there unless dragged out bodily and subjected to affection.

After several weeks, Black Jack surprised everyone. The first volunteer to arrive one morning found him waiting at the front of his cage and demanding attention. Confused and not a little suspicious, she opened his door and reached in to stroke his cheek. He leaned into her caress, then flopped over and rolled happily, nuzzling any available object. It was as though he had done some deep thinking during the night and concluded that we were his friends.

Now Black Jack was a love sponge. But he was still a plain, black, adult male in a world with too many cats. Finding a home for him might take a while. A lot of our cats end up going home with the volunteers. None of us start with the intention of adding to our family. We're all cat lovers who already have cats. But sometimes we meet one at the shelter who stays in our thoughts. Once that happens, the outcome is inevitable. The cat comes home. In February 2005, Black Jack went home with Bev.

This was the third major change in his life after arriving at his first shelter and coming to Katie's Place. It wouldn't be surprising if he went into hiding again. But although he seemed wary at first, he settled in easily and proved to be an exceptional cat.

Black Jack's love encompassed everyone he met, two-legged or four-legged. Bev's elderly, grumpy cat rejected his affections with a swat. He didn't hold it against her and continued making friendly overtures which she continued to rebuff. When Bev fostered kittens for Katie's Place, he mothered them all. One year, she fostered a skittish young female that she sequestered in the bathroom. Black Jack figured out how to open the bathroom door while she was out, and she returned to find him there, cuddled beside the cat and grooming her. Bev had all Black Jack's trust and love. Whether she was brushing his coat or rubbing his belly, he purred at her first touch.

This should have been a happily-ever-after for both of them, but events were about to take place over which Bev had no control. A family member needed to move in with her who proved to be severely allergic to cats. It was a horrible dilemma. Bev loved her cats, but her family member needed her. There was no option. The animals had to go. This is the reason our adoption contract states that our animals must come back to us if adopters are unable to keep them. People cannot envision a time when they would give up their animal, but life can unfold in undreamed-of ways.

Black Jack's second arrival at Katie's Place was vastly different from the first, more than three years before. There was no cowering and cringing. He sat at the front of his new-cat cage and greeted everyone who came in. He was twenty-two pounds of good-natured friendliness. We posted him on the web with the description Bev gave us, and he soon attracted interest. A family contacted us who happened to have an elderly, grumpy cat and wanted a cat who could handle the grump and be tolerated by him. They came to meet Black Jack, and he won them over. To a home he went again. Within a couple of weeks, we received an update.

"It was only a few days before we let Jack meet our cat. Cuddles is a tad high-strung and does not welcome competition for our affection. This was part of the attraction of what was written about Jack. He has shown all the patience you described. Jack's only desire is to be Cuddles's friend. Jack is slowly winning him over, day by day. Jack likes to greet with a good, strong head butt. He does tend to topple over Cuddles which occasionally is greeted with a few head shots. Jack just keeps on as if nothing is wrong."

We were delighted to see that this adoption was a good match, and we were confident it would last. The workers who were afraid to approach Black Jack when he arrived in shelter care that autumn of 2004 might have been amazed to see him now. It was like night and day.

"Jack has helped teach Cuddles how to be more of a community cat. Cuddles has shown Jack how to dress better and eat less."

The Hated Cat

It seemed that Felix was the scourge of his neighbourhood. He was a long-term street cat who became a nuisance to the neighbours. They turned the hose on him and threw things at him but couldn't seem to drive him off. Finally, at the end of winter 2003, they managed to live trap him, and they took him to a vet's office, saying, "Do whatever you want, as long as we don't see him again."

The vet contacted Katie's Place, and we took him. He was a long-haired, orange cat and, whatever he did to annoy the neighbourhood, he was a disagreeable-looking cat to say the least. He refused to come out of the carrier he arrived in. He lay pressed against the back of it, a brooding, orange shape with a weather-beaten face scrunched into a scowl.

Felix was obviously a hardened street cat going back many years. Aside from being grubby and ragged, he had absolutely no faith in humans. He wanted nothing to do with us, despite our attempts to be friendly. His former neighbourhood must have been celebrating his

74

absence as he lay in
a cage at our shelter,
defying us to touch
him.

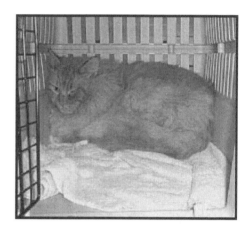

No more than a
week after he ar-
rived, we saw a sign
that his rigid defen-
siveness was thaw-
ing. We hoped he
might start to meet
our eyes and accept a caress, or venture out of his carrier.
We saw none of that. But as a volunteer opened his cage
door one day, she was taken aback to hear a thin, high,
plaintive sound like a drawn-out whimper. It was odd,
almost eerie, and it was hard to pinpoint the source right
away. It was Felix.

This was the first sign of any response from him.
His tough, street cat facade had begun to crack, and grief
spilled from the depths of his soul in that wail. It was
almost inaudible at first and continued in a long note as
though a dam that held back a flood of anguish was
breaking. The volunteer froze, never having heard such a
sound in her life. When the source and meaning hit her, it
took her breath away as the cat's suffering seemed laid
out before her. At that moment, he changed in her eyes
from a cold, defiant street cat to a vulnerable, abandoned
pet. There's nothing you can do in the face of such pain.
Caresses are pointless when an animal doesn't recognize
kindness. The human voice is an irritant.

Only time would help. Felix had to learn first, that he was safe; and second, that he was loved. It would be a slow process. Nobody had loved him for a long time. The intervening years held many instances of human hate and treachery. The memory of these had to be overlaid with enough kindness to outweigh the past. All we could do was carry on with brief, gentle approaches.

Time worked its magic. It nearly always does. Felix began to come around. Even before he left the safety of his carrier bed, if we reached in to scratch his head, he flipped onto his side, braced his paws against the wall and angled his head into our touch. He clearly enjoyed a fuss. Felix integrated into the communal room and became a confident member of the shelter community. He began to accept pets without flinching, and finally began coming to ask for them, beaming up at us shyly when we came in. By midsummer 2003, Felix was a handsome, gentle, quiet fellow who responded with pleasure to our touch.

He would need a special home. He'd never be like pets who have always been safe and can listen to glass shatter without blinking. Felix had moments when old insecurities surfaced and he became short-tempered. It didn't last long. He caught himself as he rounded on us and backed down immediately in self-conscious confusion. He knew we loved him, and he had come to love us. In January 2004, we met a family that could offer him a good home and he was adopted. We were confident they would be gentle and understanding if he had moments of insecurity. Would he hide for weeks? Would he accept life as an indoor pet? We just hoped so.

On Valentine's Day 2004, we received a note from Felix's family that put any doubt to rest. He had explored his new accommodations confidently upon arriving. For the first couple of weeks, he stayed in the downstairs area and then explored the rest of the house. He took to the teenaged son immediately and slept on the boy's bed at night. While the boy was at school, he attached himself to the lady, sitting at her side as she worked on the computer. They took him to be groomed which he seemed to enjoy. He became frisky and pounced on their legs as they walked by. His favourite plaything was a toy squirrel. He chased string, attacked newspapers on the floor, and he purred. Felix was going to be fine.

The memory of that thin, high wail will never leave us. But knowing the depths of his pain enhanced the delight we felt when reading about how well he was doing as a valued family member.

The Journey to Trust

In June 2002, four feral youngsters arrived at the shelter and crouched together in their carrier, glowering at anyone who peeked at them. They were lanky four-month-olds with ginger stripes on dark cream fur. They would have been gorgeous, but with large, kitten ears over angular faces, they looked like four angry, orange bats. We named them Humphrey, Herbert, Hank, and Houdini.

The youngsters had not received the human contact that would make them affectionate pets, and they hid from us. Through the pen wire, we saw them playing or grooming each other in a relaxed tangle of bodies. But as soon as we entered the pen, all four streaked for cover. Before they were much older, adopters came along for a pair of them. They chose the two we'd called Humphrey and Herbert, and they let us know later that the boys settled well and became affectionate surprisingly fast. No such luck for Hank and Houdini. They grew up at the shelter and considered it home.

They were happy at the shelter. The brothers knew nothing of any other kind of life. They never allowed us to touch them although they were confident in our presence and, in fact, seemed to consider us friends. The pair of them hurried over with glad faces when we arrived, and wove around our legs purring. (Of course, that probably had something to do with the canned food we gave them.) We might get away with a brief stroke of their backs. But more contact than that, and they skittered away. They didn't see enough of any one volunteer to bond with us.

Other cats were their family. The boys became adept at negotiating feline relationships. Cats from a one-pet home are intolerant of feline company. There were always a few like that in the Main Pen. They squawked in outrage if another feline invaded their space. Hank and Houdini quickly learned which cats to avoid and which ones they could intimidate. They let new cats know the pecking order and even put the run on a couple of tough street cats, letting them know for the record where they stood in seniority. They were cheerful little bounders, at ease in their world as they cruised the communal room with a swagger.

We left their posting on the web in case somebody felt equal to socializing a pair of handsome, cheeky, semi-feral boys. We made it clear that they must be adopted together since they were bonded. We didn't expect any calls. Few people want one semi-feral cat, never mind a pair. So we were surprised to receive an e-mail about the boys one day. We responded that one didn't want to be picked up while the other didn't even want to be touched, and we didn't expect to hear back from the lady. But she replied. She said she was familiar with ferals and was prepared to work with them. We exchanged several more e-mails until we became convinced that this was Hank and

Hank

Houdini's chance. Even more unusual was that the inquiry came from a small community more than 150 miles north of Maple Ridge. We don't usually do out-of-town adoptions since returning the cat could be problematic if anything went wrong.

November 29, 2004 was the day the lady drove to Maple Ridge to adopt the boys. We were nervous. What if something sent up red flags for us? We'd have to refuse the adoption, and that would not be pleasant. But her manner with the boys was gentle and assured, and they seemed as comfortable with her as they were with us. She was ready to take them home. After a half hour of trying to outmaneuver the panicked cats, we managed

Houdini

to trick each one into a carrier. Once crated, they were calm which surprised us. Even the best-socialized of cats can howl in distress when locked in a carrier. Hank and Houdini were philosophical.

Seeing the brothers safely off did not mean the end of

worrying. We hoped they could make the transition from shelter life to home life successfully. They had lived at Katie's Place for almost two and a half years, nearly their whole lives. What if they escaped from the house? Cats are diabolically clever at escaping when they set their minds to it. We couldn't even enumerate all the scenarios for disaster.

Sensing our anxiety, the lady e-mailed as soon as she arrived home and let us know the boys had traveled well and now were secured in their own room. Over the next months, she wrote regularly with updates. We expected the pair to gravitate to her other cats, perhaps never bonding completely with their human family. She was aware of that possibility and accepted it. She would be content simply to share her home with these handsome, lively brothers. We were pleased that our faith had not been misplaced. This was indeed the best thing to happen to Hank and Houdini. Without this kind of chance, they would have lived out their lives in the shelter, and they were far too young for that.

For their new family, the first challenge came when Houdini found a small hole in the wall of their room where he wedged himself. His new mom had visions of dismantling the wall to get him out. She worried that the noise of pulling off the drywall would frighten the daylights out of him. To her relief, he got out by himself. They gradually settled down, and in January she opened their door and gave them access to the entire house. When they finally dared venture out, one ran around chatting and purring while the other disappeared into hiding in the basement. Both boys were called Hankini until the family could sort out them out.

They soon determined that Houdini was the shy one and Hank was the bold one. It had been the other way around at the shelter. Hank took up residence in the basement with his brother but came upstairs every night to wander around, uttering chirpy meows. Houdini remained invisible, venturing out when nobody was around. Within a few weeks, Hank was accepting pats from his mom. He sat beside her on the couch once the young daughter was in bed and the house was quiet. But if the little girl dragged a piece of string, he chased it, forgetting caution at the prospect of a game. He was desperate to be friends with the other two cats. They rebuffed his friendly gestures though, which was heartbreaking to watch. With Houdini still in hiding, Hank's only playmates were his new mom and the child.

A month after they were given the run of the house, Hank was part of the human family and even greeted visitors. He no longer wandered around at night crying. The adjustment had been a strain though. This showed in his compulsive grooming as he licked himself bald in places. He licked his mom until she had to pull her hand away. We suggested a calming herbal infusion for both cats.

Hank began sleeping on the beds, and he initiated cuddles with his mom. "He almost sat on my lap the other night," she wrote. "He lay beside me and casually yawned, stretched, and left his front leg on my lap. Smooth move! Then he rested his head on my arm and went back to sleep."

On February 8, they had a Houdini sighting. He shot across the basement into the rafters when his mom went down there for something. She recognized the orange streak as it flew past. Ten days later, she was sitting with Hank on the couch and she noticed Houdini come up the stairs and trot casually into the kitchen. By March, he was upstairs more. His socialization progressed rapidly now and she could pet him. "He did exactly what Hank had done, which was to run past me but close enough that I could run my hand over him as he passed by. Then he ran back the other way. This went on for about six fly bys. He would look at me and purr like crazy while rubbing against a piece of furniture."

Within another month, Houdini stayed upstairs, and the brothers played such rowdy games that the family had to gather up the toys before going to bed if they hoped to get any sleep. One day at the end of March, the little girl stood still and called to Houdini who had paused a short distance away. He looked at her and seemed to debate the invitation in his mind. To the child's delight, he eventually made his way over, and she petted him as he wove around her legs.

By April, Hank was throwing himself into his mom's lap, sighing and grunting to let her know how happy he was. Houdini used his hiding places only in times of great need. He was all over people when they were seated, but ran like mad if they stood and moved. Of course he ran right in their path, so he was convinced they were chasing him for no good reason.

Soon Houdini was trying to share his mom's lap with his brother. Hank was so big that there wasn't much space left, but Houdini tried to tuck in a paw or two. In June 2005, we received our last note from the family. "Houdini now sits on my lap, and the other evening Hank came and scrunched in too. He could only get his front half in, he's so big! They were both purring like mad. It was a good thing I had two hands, because if I stopped petting and scratching for even a second, they opened their eyes to find out why."

It had taken six months, but the brothers made the transition from shelter cats to family cats. They had come a long way from the feral kittens who grew up at the shelter. They were proof that faith and patience pay off.

Where to Draw the Line?

If Keiko wasn't so beautiful, she probably wouldn't have survived. She was a Himalayan Snowshoe Siamese mix with a symmetrical triad of snowy white spots around her nose. Her face was a dark chocolate mask around large sapphire eyes. Nobody could resist her. She was adopted several times, but each adopter gave up on her. She first came to our notice when someone posted a plea on the web to save this cat's life as she'd run out of options. She lived in a community about sixty-five miles away from ours, and we didn't need any more cats. But once a volunteer learned of her plight, she couldn't get the cat out of her thoughts. She inquired.

Keiko had been adopted as a kitten and spent a year in that home until her person developed allergies. They gave her to a friend. Keiko had always been well behaved. But it was hard to be moved suddenly to another home for no reason that she could understand. The friend already had a cat, so not only did Keiko lose her own happy world, she found herself sharing another cat's world. She started peeing in the house. When her new person went on holiday, Keiko found a neighbour with no pets and decided to move in with her. Keiko's person returned and didn't seem to mind, so Keiko lived with the neighbour for about two months. Then, the neighbour started bringing a dog home for sleepovers.

Keiko started peeing in the house again. That's how she ended up at the local shelter. She was a beautiful cat and was soon adopted. Could Keiko make the transition successfully this time? The adopter was told about her problems but wasn't concerned because she had no other pets. However, it turned out that she did once have dogs in her house that peed on the carpet. By now, peeing was Keiko's pattern of reacting to stress. She lasted in that home for about six months. For Keiko, it was getting harder to trust each time.

The pretty little cat went through four homes before the age of three years, five if you include the shelter. She seemed to react to the presence of other animals, then to evidence of another animal. In the end, even a pet-free home didn't work. We were told she looked at you and just squatted as if to say "You see this? I'm mad!" A vet check found no medical problem. At the shelter, she used the pan in her cage. So they let her out with the other cats. She was fine, and they were hopeful. Then, the morning we contacted them after seeing the plea on the web, Keiko peed on the floor.

If Keiko would not use a litter pan, her only option was to live out her days in a sanctuary. Would that be fair to Keiko or the sanctuary? These were questions the volunteer put to Carol, the coordinator for Katie's Place at that time. Carol responded, "I don't care that she pees outside her box. It's a symptom. Will she ever get over it? Who knows? Should she die for it? No. Can we do anything for her? Of course we can. We can love her, care for her and protect her for as long as she needs us. If she is happy at the shelter, great. If not, we will look for a permanent foster situation where she can be accepted for who she is, flaws and all. What is the rest of her behaviour like? This will determine what we are able to offer her in terms of quality of life. Let me know."

The volunteer inquired and confirmed that Keiko was okay with other cats. Even as she wondered if any foster home would take a cat who refused to use the litter pan, Carol's words were a huge relief. This cat would be safe. We'd worry about everything else later. The worker at Keiko's shelter was equally relieved, and the transfer was arranged.

Keiko seemed to settle into the communal room at Katie's Place with no problem. She was an imperious little lady but she managed among the other cats, and she seemed to be using the litter pan. We posted her on the web with a brief history, hoping to find a no-other-pets, never-had-other-pets, adult home for her. Needless to say, we received no inquiries despite her exceptional beauty. We had lots of time to get to know her. She was bright and she was fickle. Sometimes she fell over herself to schmooze with a person, but she disdainfully ignored the majority of people who cooed over her.

Her preferences were hard to pin down, yet there was no mistaking her little antenna that perked up when a person of interest entered her area. She hurried over to her conception of the ideal lap, snuggled down and

purred
with con-
tentment.
Other
times, she
treated
visitors to
a fine view
of her
magnifi-

cent tail as she sauntered away to her favorite perch, well
out of reach, ignoring them completely. With the other
cats, Keiko was like a queen among commoners. She'd
trot past, giving a whack here and there to clear a respectful path. She loved to play. If the toys that Keiko
batted across the floor caught the other cats' fancy, they
resisted the impulse to pounce. They knew better than to
try stealing the current object of her interest.

Keiko considered the shelter home, and her litter
pan habits were faultless. Cats came and went; she
viewed them as unavoidable intrusions in her world.
With us, she was a benign little friend. We didn't force
ourselves on her or insist on picking her up. That, she
would probably not endure. Her long fur needed grooming. But Keiko considered it a personal violation when
we tried to brush her. At most, we managed a few licks
before she stalked off in annoyance. Visitors inquired but
shied away when told about her history of stress inconti-
nence. We couldn't afford to send her to yet another
home that might give up on her.

Keiko had been with us for a year when a volunteer named Karen offered take her home. Here was the home that one volunteer doubted could ever be found, either foster or adoptive. Karen was willing to take Keiko and keep her, no matter what. If litter pan issues arose, she would work through them. We knew Karen was as good as her word. Keiko went home.

We were eager to hear how she handled the transition. There was another cat in the home, and that made us more curious for news. We learned that Keiko and the other cat were civil with each other. She followed her new family around and chatted to them. She enjoyed being brushed. She quickly learned the rules of the house, such as stay off the counters, and wasn't a repeat offender. Most impressive of all, never once did she fail to use her litter box.

It seemed that Keiko was happy and fit in well. They gave her supervised outside access, and she loved to help with gardening. Every time a hole was dug, she had to look inside before anything more could be done. She ran half way up a tree one day, and her perplexity was obvious when she realized that, having gone up, she had to get down. The problem was resolved when the branch she stood on broke and she made a rapid, ungraceful descent.

Either this was the right home for Keiko, or she overcame her anxieties during her year at the shelter. Whichever, it was remarkable for a cat who'd been pegged as high-strung and unable to live with other animals. Many animals are doomed by their reputations from previous environments and circumstances. The few who are lucky enough to get a second chance usually prove how unfair it is to say what an animal will "always" or "never" do. Keiko was a rare exception who had six chances to justify everyone's faith in her.

The Rabbit Who Lost an Eye But Gained a Home

Rabbits are a misunderstood pet. They don't vocalize. They don't hug you or lick your face. This is probably why Parsley and Daisy ended up in shelter care. Daisy was gray and white and was the bolder of the pair; Parsley was brown and was the shy one – in so far as either of them showed anything of their personalities. Parsley uttered soft grunts of alarm if you tried to pick her up. For the most part, they sat motionless in their cage, side by side. They might have been more active when nobody was around. But whenever someone passed by, they were immobile, and they probably thought they'd dodged another bullet each time they managed to avoid attracting attention. We listed them for adoption, relying on their adorable appearance to interest adopters rather than their personalities. They were Dwarf bunnies, small and round with large eyes and little ears. One thing that was obvious about them was their devo-

tion to each other.
Every time we
looked in on
them, they were
pressed against
each other's
flanks.
    They didn't
seem to have
much of a future.
Nobody inquired
about adopting them. All they had was their cage and
each other. After they'd been with us a few months, we
moved them into an outdoor rabbit enclosure with a
family of young, feral bunnies. It was an experiment.
Bunnies can fight ferociously despite their meek, cuddly
appearance. But Parsley and Daisy needed more space
and stimulation, so we trialed them with the Pats, seven
identical, altered, gray bunnies who were either Patricks
or Patricias. The trial was a success. Not only did they
blend well with the Pats, Daisy particularly seemed to
embrace her new social life and could often be seen
hobnobbing with the Pats.

    They enjoyed life outdoors throughout the autumn
of 2003. Then in December, Daisy developed a sore eye,
and we put her in an indoor cage with her pal Parsley so
we could monitor and medicate her. We hated restricting
them to a cage again, but Daisy was in a bad way. The
vet diagnosed an abscess behind the eye which was
pushing it out of its socket. He tried to drain it by needle

aspiration without success, and injectable antibiotics were ineffective.

Daisy was in pain. We needed to do something. Removing the eye might work if the abscess had not penetrated the sinus tracts. The surgery and recovery would be painful, and the loss of her eye would cost her depth perception so she could never live outdoors safely again. Further, the abscess might return (bunny abscesses are a nightmare). Parsley would definitely grieve the loss of her friend if we euthanized Daisy. It was a tough decision. Do we take the chance that surgery would cure her and she could enjoy a good quality of life? Or do we let her go because of the risk and consequences if unsuccessful and hope that Parsley could deal with losing her friend?

We decided that Daisy should have the surgery. If the vet determined during surgery that her chances of good recovery were slim, then he would not let her wake up. On January 26, he began exploratory surgery. Hours later, the phone call came. Daisy had made it. He did have to remove her eye. He found one very large abscess below the eye and a smaller abscess behind it. Daisy would feel a lot better without the pressure build-up she'd endured.

It would be reasonable to wonder why we'd go to such lengths for a pet with no prospects. A common viewpoint is that the money would be better spent on the countless animals who only need minor veterinary intervention to become highly adoptable. This is something the volunteers debated among themselves from time to time as new volunteers arrived. It always came back to our mandate that we won't judge whose life is valuable. We accept as many animals as we can care for, and once they are in our care, they have our protection. Their lives have no price. Predictions of doom due to this philosophy have never come to pass. We've always been able to pay our vet bills and have not been left with a shelter full of unadoptable animals. The leap of faith we've taken again and again has been rewarded. So it was with Parsley and Daisy too. It was almost like divine intervention.

As Daisy was about to undergo surgery, we received an inquiry from someone on Vancouver Island about adopting the two bunnies. We explained Daisy's medical ordeal, and the person agreed to phone later in the week to see how her treatment had gone. It seemed the pair just might have a new home if Daisy survived. The caller was from far away though. Even local callers often find a pet elsewhere and don't call back after inquiring. But it was a glimmer of hope for the pair if Daisy recovered from the surgery. She pulled through like a champ. Parsley started grooming her as soon as she came back. The eye was sutured, and the area stayed clean. Indeed, Daisy seemed perkier and more responsive than we'd ever seen her. She cocked her head to look at us with her remaining eye, and that round, blue eye was bright with curiosity.

On February 5, her sutures were removed. The people from the Island had followed her progress and were coming the next weekend to meet the bunnies. These people were rabbit-savvy, the kind of people that are too rare considering the number of rabbits needing good homes. Parsley and Daisy would have full run of the house when their family was home and their own bedroom, which was being converted into a safe playground for them, while their family was at work. There could not have been a better home.

The pair moved to Vancouver Island that next weekend. Daisy's vet records had already been transferred to her new vet, and her family would monitor her recovery. They promised to send photos once the bunnies were in their renovated bedroom/playroom.

An update came within a week which was a pleasure to read, "The girls are doing really well. They are exploring their new environment and seem pretty relaxed considering everything. Even Daisy is running around checking things out. She is more timid than her sister, but she is already coming around. They are truly amazing."

Within two more weeks we heard that both rabbits were running around and doing bunny kicks, something we never saw them do and something rabbit-savvy people recognize as a sign of high spirits. "Parsley has been running laps around the couch as fast as she can run, and then she stops and lies out to take a break," they wrote, "then she is ready to run again. Daisy is also getting used to her surroundings, poking around, checking everything out."

In April, the rabbits went on holiday with their family. The last note we received said, "Parsley really likes to sit and relax in the sun or watch TV, and Daisy is the explorer. You would never guess that she is missing an eye. She is so outgoing and interested in everything."

Once again, pragmatists and realists among the volunteers were left shaking their heads and smiling that another leap of faith was vindicated. Two somber little rabbits who flew under adopters' radar until one became seriously ill were now in their own home, delighting their new family with joyful bunny kicks.

A Bonding of Souls

Once in a long while we meet an adopter who seems to bond with a particular animal against all odds. It may not be the kind of adoption we expect. We may wonder if it will succeed. Yet time proves it was meant to be. Quackers and Philly were lucky enough to have such an adoption.

In the summer of 2004, we were getting the usual semi-feral youngsters of kitten season. Several kittens were trapped over the summer who were too old to socialize easily. Some accepted human company in time. Others, whose horror of humans never abated, were taken to protected feral colonies. Then there was Quackers and Philly. They were absolutely terrified when they arrived. Philly huddled miserably while Quackers cried and cried until he was hoarse and sounded like a duck quacking. They were about four months old; black, medium-haired siblings with wide, angular faces beneath large kitten ears that made them look like little foxes. Eventually they accepted their new circumstances. While we were there, they stayed at the back of their condo and waited for us to leave. Only the complete disarray in their condo when we arrived told us that they played like mad when we weren't around.

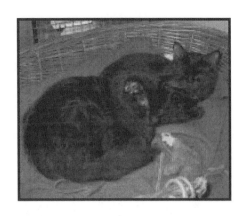

Within a short time, we were able to stroke them, a gesture they tolerated like children swallowing medicine. Finally they erupted into purrs at our touch, probably to their own surprise. Quackers soaked up caresses nonchalantly as if he'd never been scared at all. He was a bit bolder than his sister. When Philly was petted, the look on her face at first was like a student suddenly called on by the teacher, sort of a horrified "Who? Me?" Then, after a few caresses, a crackling purr started up. We listed them for adoption although we didn't expect any inquiries. It's hard to find a home for any pair of bonded cats, never mind a plain, black pair that doesn't want to be picked up and held.

When a man e-mailed to inquire about them, we confirmed that they were shy, but he was still interested in meeting them. It seemed he was looking for a pair of friendly kittens, and we hoped we hadn't overstated their pleasure at being stroked. He said he would come next weekend, and we crossed our fingers that they would let him pet them.

When we met the man, he seemed as somber and unpretentious as the kittens. The man and kittens appraised each calmly with long gazes. Then he started leaning in to pet them. They seemed undecided about whether to stay put or run, and he seemed undecided about whether to continue or back away. In the end, they stayed put and he stroked them. Haltingly, the purrs began, and in that moment an irrevocable bond formed. The man's face lit up with a smile of delight as the kittens looked up at him. They still seemed questioning, as though reserving judgement, but the man was completely taken with them. We explained about living with kittens who have a semi-feral background and their particular needs. He listened, but his attention was focused on the little black faces in front of him, and he already glowed with paternal pride. The adoption was a foregone conclusion.

We sent him home with the youngsters securely crated and told him to get in touch if he had any problems or questions. He had never raised feral kittens, and get in touch he did. He had dutifully enclosed them in his bedroom, heeding our warning that they needed to be confined for a rather long period. However, with the uncanny ability of cats to find the most improbable opening, they lodged themselves in a space above his ceiling. He e-mailed, asking what do I do now? We advised a combination of patience and trickery. They would certainly come out, given time to settle. At least, they had to come out to eat. Once he knew they were out, he should sneak in and block access to the ceiling. This was done. So they took up residence in his closet, wreaking havoc with his clothes as they came and went. Luckily he was more amused by this than annoyed. But he did seem to feel a bit wounded that they didn't return his affection. We assured him their behaviour was normal and had nothing to do with him.

We wondered if this adoption would work. He was at a loss for how to win them over. All we could advise was to give it time, and to his credit, he did. He was more than patient with this lucky, cheeky pair. Time worked its usual magic and they began to accept him.

After a few weeks, he reported, "They have now taken up sleeping in the middle of my bed, leaving me to sleep corner to corner. They're pretty well behaved when I am trying to sleep, but if they know I'm awake, they'll crawl up to me and demand to be petted. Every toy ends up underneath my couch (except for the laser pointer, that is). Quackers will now let me pick him up for a couple of moments at a time. He lasts longer just sitting on my lap, without me holding him. Philly, on the other hand, loves to be held and will sit on my lap all day and night if I let her. They follow me from room to room but will turn and run (for about a foot) if I try to get them. They do let me catch them eventually, and they both like to have their bellies rubbed."

Never once did his commitment to them waver. He was perplexed by their behaviour as they adjusted to his home. But he persisted. For reasons beyond our ken, he bonded with that skittish pair of youngsters deeply the day he met them, and he never looked back.

Four years went by and we received another note. It was a brief note which simply said, "Quackers and Philly have turned into two of the greatest joys of my life." No doubt, they adored him too.

A Brush With Death

A homeowner saw a cat crossing her yard one day with such a strange gait that it alarmed her. The animal seemed to be staggering. She called us for help. He was a long-haired, black cat in sad condition. Obviously he'd been on his own for a while. He was bedraggled, emaciated, dehydrated, and he was totally blind. He could not have survived long in this condition. Something catastrophic must have happened to him recently.

Unable to see or control his own limbs, he screamed in terror when we picked him up and took him to the vet. It was a heartrending sound, full of both fear and despair. The vet did what he could for Ray. Diagnostic tests showed some liver dysfunction and the presence of enzymes from muscle damage. The liver damage would have been the result of starvation. The reason for his other deficits was still a mystery.

In many shelters, a terrified, bedraggled street cat who is blind and badly injured would be released from this life. But the vet knew well our reluctance to deny even hopeless cases their last chance. After all the diag-

nostics were done, Ray went into foster care to be monitored.

His foster mom set him up in a cage so he wouldn't
stumble around the house. When she offered him food,
he ate ravenously. He settled quickly and seemed to rally.
Ray was not prepared to give up. We just had to wait and
see if he could recover well enough to live a normal life.

Despite his dire condition when he was found, Ray's
health improved quickly. He was no longer terrified; in
fact, he seemed active and interested. When he heard
someone come in, he made his way to the door of his
cage and sniffed inquiringly. Before much longer, his
sight returned. He followed movement with his eyes and
looked around.

The nature of his injuries and the way his functions
recovered told us how he was most likely injured. A
homeless cat is vulnerable to all manner of dangers. A
passing dog might be enough to frighten him into action.
Kids with rocks could send him into flight. The safest
retreat to a frightened cat is straight up the first vertical
surface. Unsheathed claws will carry him much higher
than good judgment would dictate in calmer moments.

Ray probably got himself stuck in a tree and, with
no family to miss him, he might have clung to the
branches for many days, too terrified to move. Finally,
weak with hunger and dehydration, his grip would have
loosened. Inevitably, he'd fall out. Too weak even to
twist and right himself in midair, as is a cat's talent, he
probably hit his head on the way down. A blow to the
head would account for the temporary blindness and loss
of motor control. He might have lain, unconscious and

unnoticed, in undergrowth at the base of the tree. When he recovered enough, he would have staggered off, driven by a will to survive. Ray was not a quitter. As he wobbled laboriously across the homeowner's property, luck was with him when she noticed him and called for help.

However long Ray had been homeless, he remembered having a home. He was a responsive, loving little guy. He greeted his foster mom when she came in, and he soaked up attention with the enthusiasm of a cat who had been alone for too long. With care and a good diet, he filled out and his coat improved. He turned out to be an extraordinarily handsome fellow. His fur was a luxuriant dark cloud, frosted with silver at the ends of his cheeks.

His temperament was equally impressive. With everyone he met, he was affectionate and gentle to a fault. His claws were probably never unsheathed after the fateful day when they carried him out of danger's reach. He slept at the foot of his foster mom's bed, and he loved a good chin rub, reaching into it with a blissful look. He never scratched the furniture. As a house cat, he was clean and well behaved. He wouldn't go on the furniture even when he was invited. He managed among the other cats in his foster home although they didn't always see eye to eye. His opinion of other cats was a minor thing in finding him a new home. Many people only want one cat. We posted him on the web and before long we had an inquiry.

Ray had become rather special to us since his ordeal; we felt protective of him. So it was a pleasure and a relief to meet the family that inquired. They turned out to be wonderful people who would give Ray a loving home. After struggling so fiercely to survive, that's the least this gentle cat deserved.

From Rags to Riches

We take cats who will never be adoptable for one reason or another. Some are feral. Some are old or sick. Some are so traumatized by the loss of their home that they never welcome another relationship with humans. These cats usually live out their lives in our care. One such cat arrived in January 2004. We called him Sparky, although it seems incongruous since he was a hulking, glowering street cat. He flattened himself into the corner of his new-cat enclosure and shrank even farther back when we opened the door to peer in at him. The only way to photograph him was to aim blindly. The results showed him pressed so far back that his hindquarters began to climb the wall. His face was a sullen mask of hatred for humans.

We didn't expect such a cat to become adoptable. He was a long-term homeless cat, plain black and white. Even if he learned to tolerate human company, he wasn't attractive. Neighbours saw him hanging around for at least a year before he was trapped, probably to their relief. The big tom was more than a little intimidating.

Weeks passed, and other cats arrived and settled in. Sparky still recoiled from us, but we finally released him from his new-cat enclosure to integrate himself into the communal room. We expected him to join the feral and shy cats who lurked in the rafters of the porch while we were around. Sure enough, he promptly made himself invisible.

Two months after he arrived, we noticed a change. While we were in the room, he stayed curled up in a chair watching us, his face inscrutable, and he made no move to run. So it goes with many cats. One kind watches from the fringes while another kind flocks at our feet. Then one morning a new figure was among the cats who gathered at our feet. We dispensed the usual strokes down each furry back. When we reached the new one in the group he looked up, and it was Sparky, experimenting with human contact.

His eyes were inquiring. They had softened from the baleful glint of two months ago. They showed a touch of both longing and sadness. We gave him a stroke as we did the other cats, and he accepted his stroke happily. He didn't feel soft or silky like his comrades. His fur was sparse, and his skin was gravelly with small scabs. Amongst his other woes, he had endured a severe flea allergy which ravaged his coat and did nothing to enhance his appearance.

Flea allergy aside, Sparky was still an unattractive cat with small eyes in a broad, pugnacious face. Often, the feel of a warm little body responding to affection will change the way they look to us. No animal is ugly who responds with love. They draw us in, and reflexively, we want to cuddle them close. But it took conscious effort to cuddle Sparky and feel the roughness of all those scabs under our hands. We listed him for adoption, but even if we had any inquiries, we knew that meeting him in person would present another hurdle toward adoption. Although he reciprocated affection, people would be put off. The flea allergy was slow to resolve. A long period of homelessness had taken its toll on his health.

In time, Sparky adjusted to life among people and turned out to be a good-natured cat who reveled in attention. What he lacked in beauty, he made up for in personality. Clearly he'd been loved once, although it had been years since he lost his home. Like many former pets who've been alone for a long time, his pent-up need for love seemed to bubble over once his defenses cracked. He was such a humble, friendly character that he became a favourite among the volunteers. When he heard the door open, he would look up with cheerful anticipation and come over for some serious schmoozing. He had become an affable little gentleman whose coat was frayed at the edges but who showed his gratitude and love.

It shouldn't have been a surprise, then, when a couple who came to adopt a pretty young tabby announced that they wanted Sparky too. They had spent a long time meeting the cats and settled on perky little Katherine as the one they wanted to take home. Being great cat lovers, they stayed a while longer to meet the others. We introduced them to Sparky as we showed them around. Making a joke of his stout build, we put our hands around him and strained as though he was too heavy to lift off the floor. He stood placidly and beamed as though he enjoyed the joke too. The couple was charmed by his ingratiating manner and touched by his story. So in December 2004, dainty Katherine and scruffy Sparky went home together. He had been with us for nearly a year, far less time than we expected.

The couple knew he was a bit of a project with his poor physical condition, and they accepted that. As they put it, they "chose not to be consumers this holiday season and to do something better instead." Sparky needed veterinary care, but with a real home now his condition improved, and he grew to be a handsome, healthy cat. The only stormy stretch when we feared he might lose this home was when he seemed to have issues with their other cats. This caused the people some anguish. They had grown to love him, but they didn't want any of their cats made miserable. However, they persevered, and Sparky kept his home.

An early report on his progress was a joy to read. He and Katherine were called Carl and Daisy. The adjustment to a new home was easy for him after everything else he'd been through in life. "Carl is very playful," they wrote, "he loves mousies (the catnip-filled kind) as well as the laser pointer, string, paper, balls.... You name it, he will play with it! He is a most amazing boy. Considering his past, he is so loving and easygoing. He was sleeping on his back last night, all fours spread out, head back, purring... bliss."

In an attached photo, there was Sparky, sprawled on his back, paws flung out, the very picture of contentment. He'd found a loving, understanding home where they adored him. Sparky was in heaven. He'd come a long way from the scowling street cat who had lost faith in humankind.

A Litany of Losses

Life becomes more precarious as we age. We begin to lose friends who were part of our lives for many years. At thirteen and fifteen years of age, Meggie and Sheba were already familiar with such loss. They had a happy home until their people moved to a facility for the elderly. The two cats lived alone in the house for about six weeks, with someone dropping by to feed them, until their fate was decided. They came to Katie's Place.

In a way, it was a blessing for them to have had that time in their old home. It gave the pair a chance to accept that their people would not be coming back before they had to face the loss of their home too. It gave them a chance to grow lonely enough that when they stepped out of their carriers at the shelter, they were purring. They had missed human company and were glad to see anyone. They purred even as they looked around uncertainly at their new environment. Sheba was a plump calico in rich colours, and Meggie was a long-limbed black-and-white cat.

The two began to settle into their new life. It's a lot to ask of elderly animals. At least Meggie and Sheba had each other. Sheba was the more outgoing one and she'd call to us hopefully from her pen. When we went in, she came to enjoy some pets. Meggie watched as Sheba nuzzled and pattered around visitors. Then she too stepped forward for her share of attention. While the visitors petted Sheba, Meggie sat close and reached out one paw, touching them lightly on the arm, looking up at them searchingly. Her eyes held a simple longing that could pierce your heart. When Sheba was satisfied and had returned to her basket, Meggie lingered at the visitor's side, enjoying affection until the very last second.

We listed the pair for adoption. But being seniors, they generated no interest. Ten weeks passed, and they adjusted to shelter life. Then Sheba appeared to be losing weight and her coat began looking rough. We took her for a vet check and learned that she had an abdominal tumour which would soon obstruct her bowels. Nothing could be done. Sheba was dying. We brought her back with pain

Meggie

medication and resolved to make her remaining time special.

We've seen many instances of cats losing their homes and arriving healthy, only to become terminally ill within a matter of weeks. It seemed to happen to chubby ones particularly. These cats may have a predisposition to a disease that would kill them eventually. What surprises us is the speed of their decline. We're convinced that if they had not endured the loss of homes and families, they would have enjoyed longer lives. If it happened every time, we would probably advise people to forget surrendering their pet to a shelter and take her straight to the vet to leave this world in the arms of someone she loves. But most seniors adjust as easily as youngsters (in so far as anyone can adjust easily to a life-changing loss).

We had posted a plea on a pet rescue message board for help finding Sheba and Meggie a home. Now that Sheba had advanced cancer, we posted a plea for Meggie. Gentle, tender Meggie who had already lost her people and home would soon lose her friend too.

Sheba's time was very short. The day she was diagnosed, we made an appointment to help her pass. But we canceled it because a volunteer took her out to the yard that day and she enjoyed it so much.

Sheba

It was spring with new growth and warmth. Sheba wandered around, lay in the sun, chased a bug, nibbled some grass, and then parked herself in front of a small animal's burrow to wait for it to poke its nose out. We hoped she would feel well enough tomorrow to come out again.

The next day was another good day. Sheba literally ran downstairs to the yard when we opened her pen door. She was so happy to toddle around, exploring the wood piles and looking for rodents to torment. She sprawled in the shade with her eyes half closed in contentment, and she greeted each visitor with a squeak, a rub and a purr. We tried giving her laxatives to clear her obstructed bowels but they didn't work. Tomorrow we would have to let her go.

Sheba was purring as she slipped away. Meggie betrayed little reaction when her friend failed to return, but she was obviously lonely. She stayed in her bed, leaving it only if someone came to visit. Then she rushed to the door. We could not find an adopter nor a foster home for her. Ten long weeks later, a volunteer who fostered high-risk cats took her home. Evelyn saved the space in her home for animals who were not thriving at the shelter. She spoon-fed cats too depressed to eat, syringe-fed orphaned kittens, and gave respite to cats who couldn't adjust to shelter life. Now Meggie was a high-risk cat.

Meggie didn't do well at Evelyn's either. She confined herself to a hidey hole where she sat primly, watching the other cats, with her tiny front feet together in their white, ankle socks and a look of disapproval on her face. Sheba was the only friend she had wanted. We were at a loss to help her. Several months later, she still had not adjusted. She purred as soon as she made eye contact with a human and still reached out with her paw, but she needed a home of her own.

In January 2005, we found a volunteer who only had one other cat, a rarity among rescuers, and she was willing to take Meggie. When Meggie arrived at Margaret's, she settled down in front of the fireplace right away, and that became her spot. The other feline, a kitten, was unruly at times, but Meggie took charge. As Margaret put it, "Think of the scene in *Raiders of the Lost Ark* when Indy's enemy is waving about the sword, making the big show, and Indy just pulls out the gun and shoots him. That's pretty much what Meggie does to the wee one when she gets a little too active – never with claws, and with a warning first."

Meggie had found her niche. One excited kitten was something she could handle. She found a home that suited her, and she put all her losses behind her. She was happy there until the end of her days.

A Fleeting Life

In 2003, another rescue group was doing regular adoptathons at the local malls. They managed to find a lot of homes this way. People only needed to see for themselves that the cats were attractive, affectionate house pets in order to dispel any concept of shelter cats as scrawny, indifferent creatures. But every now and then, a scrawny, indifferent creature was in their midst. One such cat was a black-and-white, semi-feral kitten, a skinny morsel of scruffy fur with an angular face and a wary look in his eyes. Not surprisingly, they were unable to find a home for this one, and he came to us.

He wasn't a handsome kitten at all. His most distinguishing feature was a black moustache on his white face. We named him Groucho Marx. Groucho was born into the harsh life of a homeless cat, and he had many health problems in addition to being unsocialized. He tested positive for Feline Leukemia and needed to be segregated for the time it would take to determine whether he would remain positive or revert to negative. We set him up in his own condo at the shelter where he crouched in a corner looking forlorn. There followed a difficult time as Groucho became increasingly sick. Ulcers covered his face, eyes, and the inside of his mouth. He needed several treatments daily to care for his ulcerated face, and hand feeding to maintain his nutritional status. But nothing seemed to make him better. We were reaching the point of no return with him. In the end, he went to a foster home for more intensive care. A couple of other positive cats lived there, so Groucho would at last have the feline company he desperately needed.

Despite the skepticism of our vet, we put him on interferon pulse therapy. A registered nurse in our group brought a wealth of knowledge that could sometimes be applied to the animals. Groucho slowly got better. He continued to test a weak positive to the leukemia virus, but he was growing into a beautiful, robust cat. He soon adjusted to life in a real home and became an affectionate little character.

His foster family adored him. While his future remained a question mark, we were happy that, for now, Groucho was doing well. He and his feline friend enjoyed their own version of the whack-a-mole game. Groucho hid inside a little playhouse while his pal waited outside to bat him every time he popped his head out a different window. Sometimes he just reached one furry arm out and waved it madly in the other cat's direction while keeping his head hidden. They would joust vigorously for a moment before Groucho popped out another window, catching his pal from behind.

He became an energetic, comical young cat, indistinguishable from any healthy youngster. It was a fleeting period of normalcy that wasn't to last. We've seen that the younger a cat is when he tests positive for Feline Immunodeficiency Virus (FIV) or Feline Leukemia, the less

time he has. We knew Groucho's time would be short. Yet he had become so robust and happy that it came as a blow when he developed a problem we couldn't cure. Ulcers could be treated; a respiratory infection will resolve... we treated things as they came up and carried on. But when he was about a year old, his liver began to fail. He became jaundiced until his skin was clearly yellow beneath his fur.

When the spark went out of his eyes, we knew the time had come to let him go. This was not something we could nurse him through. So his foster mom took him to the vet's for the last time. It was one of the hardest things she ever had to do, even as a hardcore rescuer from way back. He stole her heart when he made himself part of her family.

Groucho enjoyed only a year of life. But he enjoyed it to the full. He grew into a sassy young cat who claimed the world as his own. He ran up some vet bills in his one year. Had it been worth it? Yes. His one year was as meaningful as any life. After he was gone, his foster mom painted a stone with brightly-coloured images and painted his name on it. She added the stone to a special garden of memories with the stones of other animals. Knowing Groucho for his year among us had been a gift. No regrets.

A Tale of Two Sisters

In August 2004, two black-and-white kittens were
trapped and went into foster care for socializing. They
had never seen the inside of a human home before and,
at twelve weeks old, they were well on their way to
being feral. They crept around, bellies low to the ground,
slinking from cover to cover. After a while, they grudg-
ingly accepted the touch of the humans who bartered for
contact with food. One had a splash of white across her
upper lip and we called her Milkdud. The other had a
white stripe up her nose and she was called Peppermint.

They could have become adoptable but they tested
positive for Feline Leukemia, probably contracted from
their mother before birth. When they were a few months
old, they came to the shelter to live. Milkdud had begun
purring for her foster parents, but Peppermint remained
aloof. They took up residence in the Boys' Pen. After a
short period in a new-cat cage where they crouched in a
corner, faces pressed against the bars like little felons,
they were released into the population of the pen.

At first, they stayed together. We would see their little heads side by side looking down from a high nest. Soon they began mingling with the other residents. The cats became their social world and they

withdrew from the human realm, forgetting any relationships they'd forged with people in their first weeks. When we entered the Boys' Pen, they made themselves scarce.

They had no hope of adoption now. They were plain looking. They avoided humans, and they had Feline Leukemia. We didn't even list them on the web. Their lives would be spent in shelter care, and they seemed content. Being youngsters, they were active and very visible in spite of themselves. Though they wouldn't come to us for pets, we always saw them playing or snoozing among the other cats. Milkdud allowed us to touch her if we approached slowly. She enjoyed a few strokes, to her own surprise. Peppermint reserved all her affection for the other cats and formed deep friendships with individuals while Milkdud never seemed to have any one best friend.

Bonds form and dissolve among the cats much as they do among school children. Peppermint struck up a friendship with tabby Fuzzle, another semi-feral female, and they were each other's constant companion. Watch-

ing the semi-ferals together, one felt rather like Jane
Goodall among the great apes. If we kept our distance
and remained quiet, we could be privy to their lives.
They cast suspicious glances our way, and their faces
remained guarded with us. But with other cats, those
faces were alight with expression.

Whatever they did each day, Peppermint and Fuzzle
always returned to each other's side. One day Peppermint was sleeping in a little chair when Fuzzle wandered
over and lay down on a larger bed nearby. As we
watched, Peppermint sat up and looked over at Fuzzle,
her face smiling. She made her way to Fuzzle's other
side and lay down, brushing Fuzzle in greeting on the
way. Fuzzle beamed back at her. Their faces, so closed
when they looked at humans, were animated for each
other. Fuzzle leaned toward Peppermint and they nuzzled
for several moments. The gesture spoke volumes about
the comfort they found together. Their world was complete with each other's presence. Fuzzle moved closer,
and there they settled for the next several hours, pressed
into each other's flanks.

A symptom of Feline Leukemia is vulnerability to
infections, and the following summer we saw Peppermint with purulent drool on her chin. Our vet prescribed
treatment, but she resisted being medicated so vigorously
that the infection was less damaging to her than the
ordeal of treatment. We let her be, and when her mouth
didn't improve, we rounded her up for another vet visit.
The vet diagnosed faucitis – inflammation and infection
of the gum tissue. Opening and closing her mouth was

painful. She needed medication. So we segregated her in a cage and medicated her food.

Peppermint was not happy alone in the cage. She cried constantly in a high, forlorn voice. When a volunteer arrived late one evening, she found three or four of the Boys' Pen cats lying around the outside of Peppermint's cage with their paws through the bars. We asked the vet if there would be any harm to the other cats from her medication if we opened Peppermint's cage. The problem wasn't harm to them, it was getting a sufficient dosage into her. So she served her full time in segregation, and everyone, feline and human, had to bear her heartbreaking cries without being able to soothe her. When we opened the cage door at last, her mouth was better but she had concluded that our goal was to make her life miserable, and she avoided us more scrupulously than ever.

Milkdud, meanwhile, withdrew entirely from the human world. The kitten who once purred at a touch now ran at the sight of us. One day she was sleeping soundly on top of a cat post and awoke suddenly to find a human close by. She was so startled that she fell off. She caught herself halfway to the floor and clung to the post in sleepy confusion. The volunteer laughed but obligingly stepped away, and Milkdud clambered back up with a chagrined look on her face. She too developed symptoms of oral infection and had to be segregated. She didn't cry like her sister, but her opinion was obvious as she glared at us from her bed.

In June 2006, Peppermint lost her friend when Fuzzle succumbed to Feline Leukemia. She had lost friends before; death was no stranger to her. Like the other cats, she sat with them in silent sympathy as their health declined. But with animal wisdom, the survivors carried on, showing no outward sign of mourning. The losses were never sudden. The cats knew and accepted them.

Oral inflammation continued to plague Milkdud and Peppermint at intervals. In December 2007, they were confined together for medicating. Milkdud resigned herself to it while Peppermint uttered her plaintive meows of protest again. At least they had each other for company this time. When Peppermint was ready for release, Milkdud still needed three teeth removed. After her surgery, she wouldn't eat. The vet sent her home, hoping her appetite would return in her own environment. It did. Milkdud was so happy to be back, even in confinement, that she rolled and purred and greeted tabby Gordie through the bars when he came to see what was going on. Then she polished off a small can of soft food. The next day, she was sulky again. Being home was good, but now she wanted to get out of isolation.

Milkdud didn't seem to hold her confinement against us. In fact, she had a change of heart about humans. Those of us who knew her were surprised one day when a new volunteer bent and scooped Milkdud up in her arms. She nestled into the girl's neck and gave herself up to the pleasure of a cuddle. The next day, she crowded onto a lap with the other cats when a visitor sat down on their couch. She was right in the middle of the lap until she was squeezed off when Edgar sat on her. So she lay on the couch beside the visitor and cadged strokes as she wriggled and rolled with happiness. Peppermint's opinion of us did not change. While segregation seemed to persuade Milkdud that we can make her feel better, it convinced Peppermint that we like persecuting little cats.

One July morning, we watched as Peppermint joined Milkdud and Sox on the couch. At first, she didn't notice that a volunteer had left a stuffed toy in the corner. When she saw it, she was startled and jumped. Then she sniffed it thoroughly, flopped onto her side, and began playing with it. She seemed healthy and happy. But her body had fought Feline Leukemia all her life, and two weeks later she grew listless and just didn't seem well. We took her to the vet's (without much struggle which was a sign of problems by itself). There was no hope of recovery this time. On July 23, 2007, we lost her.

Milkdud continued to be friendly with us, joining the other cats for lap time on the couch. It's possible that she accepted us on their recommendation. If they were willing to pile onto our laps, she was also willing. Then on October 11, Milkdud too slipped away in a volunteer's arms at the vet's. She had been refusing treats for a week, and when she lost interest in food and her friends, we knew it was time.

The sisters were only three-and-a-half years old. Yet they had outlived other kittens who arrived with Feline Leukemia. Their short lives were happy, and knowing them as we did, we're certain that every moment was worth it.

The Feline Enigma

Randall had been hanging around a commercial district, obviously homeless. He distrusted humans, but in November 2004, a kind soul managed to trap him and bring him to Katie's Place. He lay flat along the floor of his new-cat cage like a bottom-dwelling fish, his eyes barely visible over his bedding. With more than a passing resemblance to a monkfish, he was a stocky, gray tabby of indeterminate age with a craggy face and eyes that betrayed no emotion.

He tested positive for Feline Leukemia, and judging from his appearance, he would not be blessed with much more time in life. Once he'd had a chance to settle in, we let him loose in the Boys' Pen. Whether or not he had adjusted to his new environment, we couldn't say. He was completely inscrutable. But after we opened the cage door, Randall vanished into the room and was rarely seen again. We searched him out now and then to make sure he was okay. He reacted enough that we knew he was alive and thriving. Otherwise, we took his hint and left him alone. We had to monitor him. If his time was to be short, we needed to know.

Randall didn't deteriorate. Nor did he recover. His eyes got worse, if anything. They were inflamed and weepy, and we wished we could get ahold of him and treat them. But Randall wouldn't have any part of it. For him, conjunctivitis was preferable to human contact. How long could this poor cat have left anyway? Why stress him in his last months? We let him be and got used to seeing him peer at us – if, in fact, he could peer – from the corners he retreated to when we were around.

So it continued for many months. Randall's eyes improved now and then, but even at their best, he had a cockeyed squint. Sometimes his tongue would stick out. The total effect was as unwholesome as could be. He looked like a cartoon character and could have been the model for Berke Breathed's Bill the Cat. His distrust of humans never abated, and there was nothing we could do for him without inflicting more trauma.

While he feared humans, Randall loved the other cats, and we saw him in their company more and more. He gained enough confidence to stay among his friends even when we were in the building. If we entered his room, he excused himself from the group and exited. But his bond with them was apparent. It seems that the more the cats reject human company, the more they gravitate to feline company. His friendships among the cats were important to him.

By October 2006, Randall had been with us for nearly two years, exceeding our expectation of his life span by nearly two years. He was still a peculiar-looking cat, as much due to his build as his infirmities. His ears were wide spaced and uneven. His head was broad and so flat you could rest a plate on it. The animals were oblivious to appearances, of course. They accepted him and he accepted their flaws too. In fact, his relationship with one scarred cat was the first sign of how tender Randall was behind his lopsided, inscrutable expression.

We began to see him with a cat named Bootsy Boy who had arrived with the side of his face sheared off, possibly by a vehicle tire. Bootsy's face healed. He had enough skin left to close the eye on his damaged side, but his eye would always be crooked. Bootsy wasn't feral and accepted attention from us. He was a low-key, independent fellow though.

One day, we noticed Randall leaning into the basket where Bootsy lay. Bootsy licked his head while Randall bent into the caress as though receiving a benediction. Another day, we saw Randall sitting beside Bootsy in the basket, and Bootsy was grooming his head thoroughly. Randall was pressed against Bootsy, clearly enjoying the attention. If Bootsy got distracted and slowed down, Randall leaned closer, a subtle reminder to Bootsy to continue. When the grooming was finished, Randall rested his head against Bootsy's shoulder with his eyes closed in the most touching picture of trust and affection we'd ever seen. Bootsy Boy was Randall's hero.

For quite a while, wherever Bootsy went, Randall was right beside him. Bootsy was patient with him. Randall never reciprocated by licking him back. It was the unequal relationship of mentor and follower.

In order to be with Bootsy, Randall had to accept us. Bootsy didn't fear us, and when we sat on the couch with him, Randall stayed at his friend's side. Before long, when the cats clustered around us, hungry for attention, Randall was with  them, silent, motionless and expressionless like an enigmatic little gnome. He wasn't there for our attention like the others. He was just with his friends. After a few months, we found that when we doled out strokes, we could run a hand down Randall's back too without causing him to leave. Randall never hurried. That would be too close to exhibiting emotion. When he left, he just quietly walked out. Now though, he accepted our touch. True to his nature, he never showed a reaction. He merely allowed it to happen.

At last we were able to get his eyes treated. In July 2007, we bundled him into a carrier and took him to the vet. Whether he would have bolted if we hadn't used stealth to grab him, we'll never know. He didn't acknowledge our presence when we grabbed him, and he didn't react when confined. Our vet did a full checkup while he remained as unresponsive as a stuffed toy. In August, the vet did a full-mouth extraction to deal with his bad teeth and oral inflammation. Throughout the clinic visits and treatment, Randall was stoic. The most dramatic thing he had ever done since we met him was stand and leave.

We tried to penetrate Randall's reserve. Once when he was sitting by the heater, we called his name from three feet away. He never looked up. He did stir himself; he turned around to toast his left side and let his right side cool off. But he never made eye contact. It was as though human noise wafted over him, leaving him untouched. Only by getting down at floor level, inches away from him, could we look into his face. Even then, he didn't meet our gaze. Yet we'd seen him interact with the other cats, showing such love and vulnerability. He saved it for his most trusted friends.

We moved to the new shelter in November 2008, and if Randall felt any reaction to the move, he never let it show. He had seen many changes and had outlived several friends. This was just one more. He carried on as always, perching out of our way and looking down like a squat little gargoyle. By now, we had no doubt that Randall would take his joys and sorrows to the grave. We knew he had his passions. A volunteer even claimed that she once saw him playing. Allowing that glimpse, however, was a mistake Randall never repeated.

Life continued in the old, familiar routine at the new shelter. Then one morning, a volunteer arrived to find that Randall had passed away during the night, curled up in a nest. It was March 12, 2009. He'd been with us for more than four years and was indecipherable to the last. Only other cats, his beloved friends, ever knew the real Randall.

The Cat Who Waited for His New Family

Theo was a sensitive soul. He was a large, black-and-white cat with fine, angular features. He arrived at his first shelter as a surrender. The loss of his home devastated him and he withdrew into himself, too heart-broken to accept anyone's friendship. Confinement in a cage became more and more stressful until he began lashing out. His first shelter gave up and, deemed unadoptable, he came to Katie's Place.

Arriving in shelter care is always harder for surrendered cats. They lose a home in which they were at least comfortable if not happy, and end up detained in an alien environment. They're bewildered and frightened. Stray cats, on the other hand, arrive hungry, cold and plagued by parasites. They soon realize that they now have full tummies and warm beds, and no longer feel the torments of neglected health. In no time, they're greeting us happily.

Theo had grown de-
spondent at his first shelter,
and he didn't do much
better at Katie's Place. For
many weeks, he didn't
leave the box where he
slept. Every time we
peeked inside, a pair of
somber, yellow eyes met
our gaze without a flicker

of response. His face had a grim expression, neither
sadness nor resignation. This was his life now, and there
was nothing he could do about it.

Eventually, he did come out of his box, expanding
his new world to include the communal room. He never
played, and he wouldn't mingle with the other cats. He
didn't look to us for friendship either. Theo seemed to be
morose by nature, one of those cats for whom happiness
is quiet meditation. By the end of March 2004, eight
weeks after he'd arrived, he had settled as well as he
probably ever would. He liked to curl up in a nest and
watch the daily activities with his earnest, humourless
gaze.

Open hours at the shelter are usually busy with
many visitors. Some of the cats welcome the crowd as a
chance to get more attention. Others go into hiding until
the bustle dies down. Theo was always noncommittal
about visitors. He ignored them, and they ignored him.
The friendly cats kept people busy enough. Then one day
in April, visitors went into the Main Pen where Theo
lived, hoping to meet a cat to adopt. Before we knew it,

Theo was at their feet and they were patting him. We were surprised by his uncharacteristic sociability but pleased that he seemed to be getting better with people. He wove around their feet, brushing their legs with his flanks, his tail held high in welcome. A soft purr rose from his throat. The people smiled and stroked him. We expected them to move on soon, and we would show them more cats who answered their description of what they wanted, cats less timid and sensitive than Theo. But without looking further, they decided Theo was the one. They liked him. He liked them. They just clicked; it was a done deal. We completed the adoption and crossed our fingers that Theo wouldn't revert to his withdrawn state once he was in a new environment.

Within a couple of weeks, we received a note from the family. We opened it with dread, fearing news that Theo was refusing to come out of hiding and must return. But inside were photos of Theo cavorting with a string, and sprawled on his side enjoying a tummy rub. His new name was Rupert, and his new family wrote of how much they loved him. We hardly recognized this playful, outgoing cat as Theo. Whether he had finally been ready for a new life or was waiting for those people with some unfathomable intuition, we'll never know. But the adoption was a mutual decision made by both the cat and the humans. It was meant to be.

We saw his people again several years later and learned that Theo remained an important and much-loved member of their family.

A Tale of True Love

Some animals are hard to decipher and remain
enigmas to us, but others show their feelings and opinions with childlike transparency. Kato and Brewster were
of the latter type. They lost their home at the age of
twelve when their family moved. Their people delivered
them during the bustle of our open hours, each cat sitting
in an open box, looking around uneasily. We hurried to
prepare a new-cat cage but needn't have worried. The
orange-and-white one, Brewster, was content to stay in
his box, and the little black one, Kato, was too frightened
to leave hers.

For the first several days, Brewster sat at the front of
their cage and watched everything with calm dignity
while Kato hunched miserably in the box she arrived in,
seeming to hope nobody would notice her. Every now
and then, she peeked over the rim to see what was going
on. As seniors, they lost their home at a hard time of life,
and we only hoped they would adjust and accept our
friendship. Brewster seemed to enjoy attention. Kato was
the biggest worry since she seemed so timid.

Then one day a volunteer was working in one of the pens when she heard a short "aow," almost like a chirp. It was loud as though someone was trying to attract attention. At the second "aow," she looked around and saw Kato beaming at her from their condo. For the first time, Kato was asking for attention. The volunteer went into their condo and Kato was beside herself with happiness.

No longer just a scared pair of eyes peeking out at us, she proved to be an affectionate little imp who nuzzled her visitor and strutted with a high, dainty step. Brewster sat on the sidelines watching her indulgently. Before long, he too came over and looked up in shy request, wanting some pets too. When they'd had their fill of attention, he sat down beside her and licked her tenderly.

She was a pretty cat with perfect, even features and a soft, smokey coat. A flighty little thing, she was given to emotional extremes. She went from huddling in abject fear to dancing in an exuberant show of affection. Once she felt secure, she

greeted us each day with kittenish enthusiasm. She craved affection. They both did. But Brewster was more self-controlled. While Kato was a butterfly in personality, Brewster was a rock. He wasn't handsome. He had the angular face of an older cat, with a squared muzzle and prominent chin. But he had a sterling character – stout-hearted and dependable. And he was utterly devoted to Kato.

He seemed to know she was sensitive and he watched over her protectively. From the moment they arrived when he stood guard at the front of their cage while she hid, and for as long as we knew them, he looked out for her. They often sat side by side on the same perch, watching activities around them. Every now and then, he would lean over and give her a few licks on the head. She accepted his love without question and seemed content knowing he was there.

Obviously they had to be adopted together, so the odds of them finding a new home were slim. Most people don't want to adopt a senior pet. Probably the only pet more unpopular than an aging animal is two aging animals. We expected to have this pair for a long time. It was sad because they wanted a family so much. Whenever we visited with them, they pressed close, nuzzling, purring, and licking our hands.

During open hours when the shelter grew noisy and crowded with visitors, Kato soon decided it was far too busy and retired to a cubby hole. Brewster sat on his perch and watched, unshakable as ever. If anyone showed interest in them however, even Kato could be persuaded to come and greet her admirers.

Noble Brewster, and flighty Kato – everyone was enchanted by them but nobody wanted to adopt them. Time passed and they regarded us as their family, showing us all the affection they would have offered a family of their own. They were a favourite among the volunteers. We are in the enviable position of knowing the animals intimately and can choose a furry companion with that knowledge. Eventually one of the volunteers decided to adopt them. In May 2005, five months after arriving at the shelter, they went to a new home.

Before long, their proud new person brought photos to show us along with a report on how they were doing. Her note described their adjustment to her family. "On their first night at our house, Brewster thought our dogs were going after Kato (they weren't). So he ran after the dogs (a German Shepherd and a Rottweiler), hissing and spitting. The dogs were terrified. Both the cats are getting used to the dogs now, and vice versa."

We weren't surprised to hear of Brewster's reaction to the dogs. If he thought they might hurt Kato, he would act, despite his gentle personality. We knew Brewster would have faced the most formidable foe to protect his beloved Kato.

Putting Memories Away

While strays can find shelter life an improvement, it's hard for surrendered cats to end up at a shelter. Sometimes the only positive aspect for a surrendered cat is that he wasn't really wanted in his old home. Coming into shelter care is hardest of all for cats who were cherished. We've seen cases where they faded and died after losing their home, despite all efforts to help them. The longer they had the home, the harder the loss. It's a tough adjustment, but they can adjust. Cheech was a ten-year-old who lost his home suddenly, a home he loved and where he was loved.

He arrived at the shelter in June 2005 when his person went permanently into care. He was a large cat with a white undercarriage and a dark-orange saddle. Sleek and healthy, he had clearly been cared for well. He could not understand what had happened when his person disappeared and he was taken from his home. The shock of it showed in his face as he lay flat in his new bed, chin on the ground, eyes grim, as though he was willing the earth to open up and swallow him. He stayed that way for some time, unable to respond to any friendly gestures. All he could comprehend was the life he'd lost. If that was gone, he had nothing. There was no future. He couldn't even lift his head.

Two or three weeks later, we considered it encouraging progress to find Cheech sitting up even if the look in his eyes was still wounded disbelief. Progress continued in small degrees as he sat up one day, then looked out at the world beyond his cage the next day. His face remained somber and his eyes, distrustful. He might have been the kind of cat who retreated to a back room when the doorbell rang. Now he had no choice but to live surrounded by strangers. One time, he sat staring with an intense and unfocused gaze as though watching something inwardly, trying desperately to keep it in view. Animals have memories, and Cheech surely remembered the past with poignant sadness.

All we could do was make sure he kept eating and give him time. He lived in a new-cat cage for quite a while. His appetite was sketchy, and if a large, older fellow like Cheech stopped eating, he could succumb to Fatty Liver Syndrome. Cheech didn't mind the confinement. He had no desire to move around anyway. In time, he seemed to reach a stage of acceptance. He was eating and grooming, even if he was still dour. Such animals need a new home as badly as it is hard to find one for them. Nobody wants a sullen cat who won't respond to them. Few people can imagine that such a cat has any potential. Still, we introduced Cheech to people, and one day in January 2006, it paid off. A family decided to adopt him. He showed enough promise that they wanted to give him a chance. He was lucky they had faith. It seemed as though Cheech still believed his real home and person were out there somewhere, and he had trouble accepting any other. But eventually he did begin to look forward rather than back.

In September, they sent us a note saying, "Perhaps because he's a bit older, he took a few months to really warm up and trust us, but now he's very friendly and likes to be wherever we are in the house. He enjoys being petted and played with and now accepts being picked up. His specialty is lolling around in cute poses and thumping his tail like a Labrador. Thanks for helping us choose the right cat, and continue encouraging folks to adopt a senior. They are loving and lots of fun."

However devoted he was to his first person and first home, Cheech had managed move on. Almost three years later, we heard from the family again. "He remains a beloved member of our household," they wrote, "and since March, has been our only cat. He truly is a sweetheart, lovely and gentle with a beautiful, plush coat and very clean habits. He keeps himself in shape by climbing up and down the stairs many times a day between the main floor and the upper landing where his food bowl is kept. He also keeps us amused with a game he invented which involves repeatedly leaping in one bound down four stairs to the lower floor and then racing around.

We were less amused when we discovered he was using these strengthened leg muscles to leap onto the kitchen table and counters in search of snacks (preferably any sort of bread, muffin or bagel). We are so glad to have been matched up with him and appreciate your efforts to find the right cat for our household. He remains rather timid with strangers at first, but eventually comes around to check them out and is obviously very content and happy. Friends find it almost impossible to believe that he is thirteen years old as he seems so youthful and not at all like an old fellow."

The image of Cheech prowling the counters for baked goods made us wonder if maybe his first person had shared snacks with him. Perhaps that was a happy ritual he flashed back to in his bleak days at the shelter. Whatever memories he had, Cheech was able to put them away and enjoy a new life.

Fowl Play and the CFIA

Katie's Place usually has just cats, occasionally
some rabbits. But over the years, we've rescued a variety
of small animals in dire need. We would make room in
any way we could when an animal faced premature death
without our help. That's how we came to have Sonny
and Cher.

These two little black chickens were refugees from
a packing plant. The first dilemma they presented was
where to put them. We had a fenced backyard, but they
needed protection from predators. There was the large,
covered rabbit enclosure, about ten feet by twenty-five
feet. At the time, it housed seven or eight rabbits and
certainly had room for a couple of small chickens if the
two species could live together. We decided to trial
Sonny and Cher in the rabbit pen.

The rabbits didn't mind their peculiar new roommates, and the chickens were nonchalant about the rabbits. They cohabited nicely, so well in fact that when a
duck arrived, we put her in there too. The whole group
was a fine example of tolerance. The rabbits had their

hutches, and the birds set up house-keeping in an old doghouse we'd placed at one end. Otherwise, they intermingled nicely.  The rabbits turned out to love the feed we threw down for the birds. At dinner time, every creature in the pen hurried over as we tossed out the grain. Gathering in a circle around it, they munched with gusto, birds and bunnies side by side. As long as it didn't hurt the rabbits, we saw no harm in it. There was enough feed to go around.

The one distinction among the species was that Gwyneth Poultry, the duck, was the only resident who showed any interest in the tub of water we provided for her. The chickens and rabbits chose not to join her there.

We monitored the health of each creature and sometimes had to single one out for closer examination. This involved trailing them around the enclosure until we were in a position to grab them. It sounds easier than it was. Most of the rabbits were feral. Those that weren't might as well have been for all that they welcomed our company. Unless we came bearing food, they had little use for us.

Of course, the birds stayed a wary distance from us. All the enclosure's residents kept us under close observation when we were on their turf. Sonny and Cher maintained a running conversation as they watched us move around, and their preoccupied clucking rose in volume if they became separated. It was as though they were calling moves to each other, aiding each other in avoiding us.

The best place to corner an animal was a narrow corridor between the wire fencing and the back of the hutches. Birds and bunnies alike headed into this corridor, hoping to lose us, and became a traffic jam that bottlenecked in the narrow passage. The bunnies shifted impatiently and the chickens clucked in annoyance as they all jostled to keep moving. If we reached down to collar an individual, that created a panic of flapping wings and stamping feet, and usually they all wriggled away in the confusion before we could nab anyone. It was a blessing that we rarely had to collar an individual.

Over time, Cher laid an egg or two in their doghouse home. Evidently she wasn't a laying hen, or if she was, she was spent because she never laid more than a couple of eggs in the time she was with us. They were not destined to hatch, and Cher abandoned them to carry on her perambulations around the enclosure. Sonny, however, was thrilled with the eggs and sat on them conscientiously for hours, protecting them with admirable paternal devotion. He never seemed to notice that they didn't hatch. He was just proud to have an egg. Cher turned a blind eye to Sonny's paternal behaviour just as she did to the eggs. The nonviable and the eccentric were both best ignored in her opinion.

The birds had only been with us for about a month
when a threat to their lives came in the form of the Cana-
dian Food Inspection Agency (CFIA). It was April 2004.
Sonny and Cher were certainly not food, not in our eyes.
No animal in our care was ever to become food. But an
outbreak of avian flu on commercial farms caused panic
among poultry producers. The CFIA's response was to
eliminate the disease by eliminating birds. Entire farms
were cleared of chickens as each and every bird was
slaughtered and discarded. It was a terrible loss for the
farmers. The crisis and the solution terrified people with
pet birds and small, backyard flocks. They feared their
birds would be seized and killed whether or not they
were sick.

Carol, the shelter coordinator at that time and a
crusader at heart, united local bird lovers to fight the
indiscriminate slaughter of pet birds and backyard birds.
They signed a petition to city hall asking for help. A
photo of Carol holding a Katie's Place chicken appeared
on the front page of the *Maple Ridge Times* over the
headline, "Owners want birds spared."

We kept an eye on the CFIA website. In mid-April,
the site said they were "now depopulating the control
area, targeting first those premises where infection is
present or suspected," and we scanned a map to see if we
were in the control area. We knew Sonny, Cher and
Gwyneth were healthy and that their chances of exposure
to the virus were remote.

There were three other chickens at the shelter who
had lived there since before we arrived. The Colonel,
Carmilla, and Chicken Little had a coop adjoining the

barn and enjoyed free run of the backyard. The three of
them wandered around as an inseparable trio. So we
looked after six birds in total, and we were determined
not to let the government kill them needlessly.

The next time we checked the CFIA site, it said,
"The disease has also been confirmed on 10 smaller
premises, commonly known as backyard flocks. The
CFIA has depopulated all of these premises." We grew
more anxious for our birds. "There are now inspection
points leading out of the valley to prevent unauthorized
movement of birds," the site said. They had encountered
resistance and were cracking down. Some people feared
for beloved pets. Some bred valuable birds. Whether
they fought for love or money, people fought.

The *Vancouver Sun* covered the crisis. "Commercial
and hobby farmers surrounded the region's chief veteri-
narian, Cornelius Kiley, bombarding him with questions,
while other farmers stood in small groups, venting about
the mass cull of both infected and uninfected birds...." It
had become big news.

The CFIA held an informational meeting in Maple
Ridge on April 28 and announced that they were no
longer testing prior to killing birds. All birds would be
killed and tested later. It began to look like we might not
win this fight. But the CFIA, apparently sensing the
mood in the room, emphasized that things could change
from day to day.

We had done what we could. On May 15, we
learned that CFIA inspectors were seen around Websters
Corner, a few miles away from us. We braced for the
worst. Then suddenly it was over. The avian flu was

eliminated or contained to the CFIA's satisfaction, and our birds were spared. We removed the signage warning that birds were on the premises, and normal life resumed. Our birds pottered around the rabbit enclosure, oblivious of how we'd fought for their lives.

We had felt self-conscious about it at times. We were crusading to save a few barnyard fowl. Some might have thought we were crazy. But it came down to principle. "All life is valuable," we said in our mission statement. We couldn't fight any less for our birds than we would for a litter of kittens or puppies.

Sonny and Cher bid farewell to their rabbit roommates in December of that year when they went to live on a hobby farm. Gwyneth Poultry had already gone to a similar home. So the rabbits had to give up their chicken feed treat and resign themselves to a diet of rabbit pellets and vegetables again. This they did without showing any reaction at all to the loss of their feathered companions. In fact, neither group, fowl nor rabbit, ever betrayed any opinion of each other, or any particular appreciation for the safe haven we'd provided. But that was not why we looked after them. Their lives were precious. Period.

The Supreme Drama Queen

Some cats are so placid they could be adopted out as paperweights. Most are livelier but easygoing. Then there are a few who are melodramatic divas with larger-than-life personalities. Esmée was one of the latter group. She was a slender calico, mostly black with a white bib, who came to us from another shelter in May 2003. She was deemed unadoptable because she lashed out. Her expression was always intense. Her eyes were always wide as if everything constantly amazed her, and they were appraising eyes. She was the greatest feline drama queen we'd ever met.

We set her up in a new-cat cage, and she crouched inside her box looking grumpy. With every sound from the room beyond, she craned her neck to peek out and see what was going on. She was keenly sensitive to stimuli. No doubt, this was the root of her diva behaviour. She lived in a state of overstimulation. It didn't seem to cause any particular distress to Esmée herself, but it was a problem for those around her. When she was released from her new-cat cage into the communal room, she promptly sorted everyone out, letting cats and volunteers know with shrill yelps that they were not to violate her personal space under any circumstances. The other cats scuttled out of her way with knowing resignation. They had encountered other divas and learned to avoid them. Esmée took the coveted shelf by the door as her spot. It afforded its occupant the most inclusive view of the downstairs area and positioned them close to everyone who entered or exited. Cats on that shelf were the first to be stroked and the first to see treats arriving. No other cat disputed Esmée's claim to this shelf. A few bold ones asserted their right to sit in the surrounding area. But Esmée included that in her personal space, and they always capitulated in a scowling stare-down.

Esmée had no time for other animals, but she wanted people to like her and tried very hard to be friendly. When we entered the pen, our self-appointed greeter stood as if overcome by the expectation of something spectacular. She heralded her visitor's arrival with fanfare as she paced the shelf and nuzzled the wire until it buckled. We could give her a brief stroke or pat, which she enjoyed. But longer petting was cause for an affronted rebuke.

Esmée was a cat of extremes. Life's mundane moments were major events for her, and too many strokes were a grievous personal violation in her perception. Some people handled her more easily than others. Esmée was selective about the humans upon whom she bestowed her favour. We had to be alert during our open hours and warn visitors about her. If a stranger impul-

sively tried to
cuddle her, she
would leave
them in no
doubt about
her disap-
proval.
We didn't
expect to find
a home for
Esmée any

time soon. But in December 2003, someone did express interest in her. With her larger-than-life personality, she was a high-profile cat in the Main Pen, and people were amused by her. The adopters saw Esmée's nature for themselves as she dispensed small measures of good will to the humans around her and flapped hysterically at any cat who tried to steal her limelight. They were prepared to give her the space and time she needed. We believed that in a real home with more room and fewer cats, she could do well. So Esmée was adopted.

Apparently, we misjudged either Esmée or the adopters. After a few days, in which she traumatized the family and their other animals, she was returned. Perhaps Esmée had adjusted to the shelter more than we realized when they met her. Esmée in new-environment mode would be a formidable experience for the uninitiated. She was upset to find herself deposited back in the Main Pen. For a few weeks, she was more prickly than ever. She reclaimed her shelf by the door and gradually settled back into her routine, cadging attention from chosen people.

One day a couple of volunteers were chatting through the wire at the Main Pen door, one outside and the other inside. While they talked, Esmée reached over from the shelf and placed her front paws on the inside volunteer's chest. The volunteer continued talking and absent-mindedly rubbed Esmée's head and ears. She was purring and rubbing her cheek against the volunteer's chin when the volunteer stopped short and asked, "Who am I petting?" She couldn't see the cat's face that nestled under her chin. When she heard the reply, "Esmée," she slowly disengaged the paws from her chest and backed away. She didn't want to be that close when Esmée reached her limit.

Another volunteer once complained that Esmée shredded his rubber gloves every week when he tried to reach past her while cleaning. Somebody observed that maybe Esmée didn't like rubber gloves and suggested taking them off to see what would happen. The volunteer dryly declined this suggestion that would pit his unprotected hands against Esmée's claws.

In January 2005, she developed a cold that didn't seem to go away. Not surprisingly, nobody wanted to try syringing antibiotics down her throat. We thought it best to segregate her and put the medicine in her food. So into a cage she went for the duration of her recovery. The evening ritual of mushy food was almost sacred to Esmée. She was always ready and waiting on her shelf for her own plate. We suspected that even though she was unhappy about being caged, she would devour her dinner, medicine-filled or not. Fortunately we were right. She finished her medication without problems, and we left her cage door open. But she had grown to like her own private suite. She snoozed inside the cage for a further week before reclaiming her shelf.

By May 2005, Esmée had mellowed considerably. She loved hugs and would stand on her shelf clinging to people with her front paws. She even enjoyed being held. As long as there was no bustling nearby, she could be as sweet as sugar. But underneath that docile exterior, there still lived a feisty diva with a short fuse. She was in the middle of a hug one day when a group of people entered the pen. The activity behind her unsettled her and she kept looking around to see what was going on. Her patience soon burned out, and she scrambled away from her surprised friend with a shriek. Yet, a few minutes later, when everything was quiet again, she was back giving hugs.

Esmée longed for affection from a person of her own. So we were receptive when, in June 2005, one of our cat-savvy foster parents took an interest in her and offered to adopt her. We talked it over with the lady, and Esmée went home on foster status to see how she would adjust. A lot of time had passed since her failed adoption. She was a gentler Esmée now. It was worth a try.

Within a few days, we received the first report. "Esmée went on full house inspection. She was not too impressed with all the different smells of cats around and went under my bed. In the morning, all bowls were clean, she found the litter box and used it, and she greeted me with a luxurious stretch. She's a lovely little lady. She comes, ready to be petted – not at all shy." We still weren't entirely convinced of Esmée's conversion though. We waited a few more days, and another report arrived. "There are no fights. She is behaving. Her favourite place is the window sill looking into the garden. The tip of her tail quivers when she sees me. She trusts me. I brush her every day, and she sleeps in my bedroom with the other cats present." If the first few days had gone so well, it looked like Esmée's fortunes had changed. On July 3, we finalized her adoption.

Against all odds, this little diva had found her niche. Three years later we received our last update. Apparently Esmée still preferred to avoid other cats. She now had her own bedroom. In a world where even humans often share a room, Esmée would still consider this her due.

The Cat Who Sang

Gibby was a black-and-white cat with a black patch below her mouth and white above it. This demarcated her mouth so her smile showed from across the room. Gibby was usually smiling. She was a cheerful cat by nature. But she was also high-strung and did not like other cats. She seemed to have a low threshold for stimulation. So her life became tough the moment she left the familiarity of her own home.

Finding herself caged in a roomful of other cats at her first shelter, Gibby lashed out and made herself unadoptable. In January 2005, she came to Katie's Place. From Gibby's perspective, this was not a step up since she encountered even more cats. She didn't realize it was her last chance at survival, and she expressed her displeasure in her own singular way. Gibby was a vocalizer.

She wasn't much different from any new cat during her confinement in a new-cat cage. She watched everything from the safety of her hidey hole and grumbled if anyone came too close. The drama began when we released her into the communal room. She prowled around

the Main Pen intoning her distress. Consonents and
vowels flowed together in a protracted vocalization,
something between a howl and a hum. The sound undu-
lated in volume and pitch as Gibby encountered one cat
after another. "Errarraowoorarerawoooer," she sang
almost continuously, pausing only to sniff an informative
item here or there.

"Awwooeraraer," sounded in muffled tones as she
crawled under the chair and resumed full volume when
she came out the other side. Eventually she did grow
quiet. At least, her anxious vocalizations died down to
the occasional "Erooawow" when she glanced around to
see if any cats were stalking her. Some of her roommates
looked impressed at her range of vocabulary. Some
looked scandalized. And if cats could roll their eyes,
some would have done that.

Within a few weeks, Gibby settled down. Sometimes you could forget she was there. Only when things
were hectic did she still vocalize. If the shelter became
crowded during open hours, conversation stopped dead
when the unearthly sound of Gibby's lament erupted
from wherever she was lurking. The question was written on people's faces. "What on earth is that?"

"That's just Gibby," we'd say, hoping that explana-
tion sufficed. When she wandered into view, we ruffled
her head and explained that she was harmless, just noisy.
Then people smiled and ignored her. Poor cat, it was just
as well she didn't know that people laughed at her omi-
nous wailing.

Gibby really was all talk. She meant well and was
affectionate until she reached her limit for stimulation.

Then her unmelodious utterance was her way of dealing with it. If people pushed her even after her vocal warnings, she might swipe at them, but it was more of a warning feint.

Shelter life was stressful for Gibby since she could never relax in a busy environment with a lot of other cats and people. Her low tolerance for stimulation, the language she resorted to, and the way she could feign a defensive strike all hurt her chances of getting a home. She was a bright, friendly cat who would have been fine in a real home. It was Catch-22, a no-win situation.

In June, the volunteers noticed Gibby making a lot of unproductive visits to the litter pan, and she seemed grumpier than usual. Being unable to use the litter pan can be a serious problem, so we whisked her off to the vet's where we left her complaining about the upheaval she was suffering in addition to her discomfort. She came back with the diagnosis of crystals in her urine and some medication to be taken over the next several days. Gibby was usually all talk, no action, but would she allow us to medicate her? We'd rather not have had the opportunity to find out. She was segregated in a cage, and she seemed content by herself. A brave, senior volunteer administered her meds successfully.

Five weeks later, Gibby was still segregated. We needed to monitor her diet, and the only way to do that was to prevent her access to the communal food bowls. Gibby was not pleased about this, not pleased at all. She had too much energy to be happy for long in a small enclosure. So although her bright, interested face smiled at us whenever we passed her cage, the volunteers who cleaned it faced a challenge. We heard yelps and admonishments from the cleaners as Gibby vented her frustration by rushing the door or cuffing them.

Over time, frustration took its toll on Gibby. Where any pokes she had taken at people before were mere feints, she now began making contact with some smart cuffs. Our volunteers understand cats, but even their patience was taxed by Gibby's behaviour. Since her diet needed to be restricted, we decided to put her in the smaller, upstairs communal pen where cats with a restricted diet were assembled and hope there was enough space to keep her content. It wasn't a large room. In fact, it was the smallest room in the shelter. But Gibby did seem happier. She was her old, funny self, wandering around venting tension in grumbles and mumbles, all set to her own music. But you could pet her and pick her up without getting cuffed.

Weeks passed and Gibby became restless again. It was a fine, warm summer, and she sat at the window looking out as far as she could, pleasure obvious on her face at the sight of trees and fields. When the activity level around her increased, it jangled her nerves. The volunteers became annoyed with her again because the bustle of cleaning got her wound up. Yet there was a relentlessly cheerful innocence about her. She had no idea she annoyed anyone. After venting her tension, she beamed amiably again.

One volunteer fell in love with Gibby. She had a diva cat at home, so she was no stranger to diva tendencies. The young woman was moving to another community and would be able to have Gibby in her new place.

In the
meantime,
we assigned
Gibby to
one of the
condos so
she could
have her
space and
everyone
would be

safe from her petulance. She was happily unaware that
she had a private suite because nobody wanted to be near
her.

The condo wasn't ideal for Gibby, even in the short
term. She was bored, and she had so enjoyed the summer
from the window of her communal room. One day in late
August, we put her on the upstairs porch to enjoy a little
fresh air. She seemed to like it. At least, her face was
beaming as usual. But after a while, we saw her panting
in the heat, so we ushered her into the adjoining communal room to get her out of the sun.

"Errarrarer," she muttered as she noticed other cats.
"Owwooarrerraerr" she continued as she found she
couldn't put enough space between herself and them.
The cats ignored her. But she continued expressing her
vexation, and then she whacked a volunteer on the ankle.
So back to her single cage she went.

Gibby's adopter came to take her home at the end of
August and the adoption was a relief to everyone. Her
new person had waited until the details of her move were

finalized. Then she collected Gibby and drove off for the last time, and we wished them both well. At least this volunteer knew Gibby and knew exactly what she was getting. A week later, we received a note from her. "Things are going just fine with Gibby. She's settled in way better than I expected and could even be called well behaved. I always suspected that deep down she was a nice cat, and now I have proof. She's a complete sweetheart!"

A few weeks later, we received a last note. "She can be a brat, but I think she more than makes up for it just in the number of times a day she makes me laugh with her weird little quirks, like flinging herself at me to attack my ankles when I'm wearing long pants. (It's probably something she ought to get in trouble for. But she doesn't bite hard at all, and it's just so funny.) There's also one sweatshirt of mine that seems to have a magnetic attraction for her. Whenever I'm wearing it near her, she gives a little chirp, bites down gently on my sleeve, and holds on. It's the weirdest thing. We're having such a great time with her. She is the most playful cat I've ever seen!"

Poor, dear Gibby was and always would be an eccentric character. Lovable but eccentric. Luckily, she found someone who appreciated that in her.

The Cat Who Fought to Trust

One of our volunteers also gave time at the municipal shelter and met most of the municipality's stray cats there when they were turned in. Some of them came to Katie's Place if they weren't claimed and weren't adoptable. Many of those became adoptable, given more time and care. But a few would never find homes. Either feral or damaged in body or spirit, these cats would live their lives out at the shelter, in foster homes or feral colonies. These cats were the exception, a small percentage of all that came through the shelter door.

One day, the municipal shelter accepted an orange-and-white cat who looked like he was in that small percentage of cats who will never come around. He crouched at the back of his cage, a large, grubby male with tattered ears. His face was bloodied from trying to bash his way out of a trap. He squinted at the volunteer with the aversion that ferals show for the human species when they've been trapped and taken from their homes. Even a cat lover would have had a hard time feeling sympathy for this dirty, malevolent-looking creature. The volunteer left him alone. That was obviously what he wanted.

The cat was still there two weeks later and still looked as furtive and spiteful as ever. By her next visit, he was gone from the cat room, and she suspected the worst with a twinge of regret for him. But when she went to the back room where cats who developed upper respiratory infections were housed, he was there, trying to hide in the corner of his cage. He had a different look though. He seemed less malevolent, and a hint of vulnerability showed in his face. She paused in front of his cage and talked softly for a few moments to see what he'd do. He recoiled into a ball, but he never looked away. The big stray gave no other response, so she turned and headed for the door.

As she grasped the door knob, an urgent wail came from one of the cages behind her, like the cry of an unhappy child. She turned back to see which cat was crying with such distress. It was the orange-and-white stray himself. He had moved forward in his cage and was watching her, anguished with yearning and loneliness. He was asking for attention he could hardly bring himself to accept. Surprised, she went back. He still shrank away. But she could see him struggling to overcome his mistrust. Maybe there was potential here.

He was still in the back room when she next visited. She opened his cage door and reached in to stroke his head (which no longer seemed a dangerous thing to try). He flinched at the touch, but he crept closer despite his fear, wanting love and reassurance. Staff gave him the improbable name, "Goody Sam," and "Goody Sam" he

remained when he came to Katie's Place in October 2004. He hadn't come around enough to interest adopters. He needed time to struggle through his fear and move toward people. Visitors glancing at him saw only an unappealing cat and moved on to see cats who would respond immediately.

Goody Sam was still an unknown quantity at Katie's Place. He might become one of those cats who live on the fringes, accepting pets when offered but never seeking them, and never attracting adopters' attention. However, he surprised us. First he leaned tentatively into a loving touch. Then he reveled in it. He rolled over and pressed his head into our hands, his forepaws kneading the air as he abandoned himself to the pleasure of a fuss.

It became the norm that when we arrived at the shelter, Goody Sam's face was one of the first we saw as he anticipated a visit. That face, which once looked so defeated, now glowed with cheerfulness and trust. He loved us. He loved being loved. He finally forgot the horrors of living homeless, hated by people whose gardens he trespassed. This sensitive animal became one of the most affectionate cats in his pen. He also became clean and handsome now that he no longer slept in culverts and survived on garbage. It was inevitable that somebody would fall in love with him. In November 2005, a year and two months after he came into shelter care, Goody Sam was adopted. His story epitomized the hope that keeps us coming back, despite frustrations or heartaches.

A Grumpy Old Lady

Tasha was a dainty, long-haired tabby who was surrendered to the municipal shelter. She was ten years old. As an older cat, her chances of being adopted were poor, and new animals continued to stream into the shelter. So in June 2004, she came to Katie's Place. She was a perky little cat but, like other seniors, she had limits to what she'd tolerate. She'd let you know when she'd had enough with a snarl and a swipe.

She wasn't happy with the move to Katie's Place since it put her in the midst of a whole new group of strange cats. Tasha had no wish to be anywhere near other cats. She coped by taking up residence in a high, covered nest on the porch. She was calm and responsive when we checked on her, but we had to put food in there because she wouldn't even come down for meals. Still, with a bit more time to adjust, she did come out. The old girl stationed herself on the north-east corner of the ledge on the Main Pen porch. That was her spot, and other cats understood that they were not welcome there. Humans were another matter.

Tasha welcomed everyone who arrived at the shelter from her spot on the ledge which was closest to the entrance.

When cars pulled in, she stood in anticipation. As people got out of their cars, she waited for them to come up to the wire. Then she circled back and forth with remarkable grace and agility on that narrow surface, and she nuzzled the wire with enthusiasm. That was where she preferred to conduct her social relationships. She was not interested in you once you entered the Main Pen. If you tried to visit with her inside, she was indifferent and would cut the visit short with an impatient swipe, seeming to forget that you had been her lauded friend five minutes ago.

She abandoned her post on the porch during a cold snap that winter. When it was well below freezing, she didn't care who arrived. The Greeter was off duty. Find your own way in. She chose to curl up inside the shelter and snooze away the dark winter afternoons. Spring saw her resume her post outside and begin greeting visitors again with the old fanfare.

In May, she developed a minor eye infection, part of a common upper respiratory virus. Tasha looked delicate, but if you underestimated her strength and stubbornness,

it was at your peril. Medicating her was as damaging to
both Tasha and the volunteers as letting the infection run
its course. She simply did not allow it, not without a
huge uproar. Yet if we spent a little time with her when
she felt mellow and receptive (and when we didn't have
to medicate her), she purred and let us scratch her head
while she licked our fingers.

Tasha missed having a real home and a person of
her own. She avoided mingling at the shelter and glowered at the world, making herself unattractive to
adopters. There weren't enough homes for all the affectionate youngsters, never mind an eleven-year-old with a
low tolerance for being handled. We didn't know what to
do for her. Living out her life at the shelter was a bleak
prospect.

Evelyn, the animal health volunteer, had Tasha on
her mind. The old cat hadn't seen the vet since arriving
at the shelter. As a senior, she needed monitoring. But
she was not amenable to being picked up and checked
over. We had managed to medicate her before. However,
the window of opportunity was small. Now she needed a
checkup. Her coat had become matted, and brushing was
not an option. It was time to get her in. So Evelyn
scruffed her, popped her in a carrier, and headed for the
vet's with Tasha's outraged protests filling her ears. Vets
work their own magic with uncooperative animals, and
Evelyn left it to them to remove her matted fur in any
way they could.

When she returned to collect the animals she'd left
for checkups that day, she was amazed to hear the vet's
story. Tasha had been as good as gold. She allowed her

coat to be brushed, and a sweet-natured Tasha now greeted Evelyn. She had intended to foster the old cat after the vet visit since she seemed so unhappy at the shelter. She did go home with Evelyn, and her new mellowness continued. Evelyn reported that Tasha would still let you know when she'd had enough. Otherwise she was good-natured and easygoing; completely different from the little grump we knew in the shelter.

In October, Evelyn had to leave town for a while and the plan was for Tasha to stay at the shelter until her return. But one of those rare miracles occurred – an adopter came looking for a hard-to-place cat. The lady wanted a cat who really needed a home, and the cat would be her only pet. Tasha was an obvious candidate. The adopter met Tasha, who was not exactly gracious. She dismissed her visitor with an irritated swat, the same way she dismissed all of us. Luckily for her, the lady understood that she was stressed, not aggressive, and wanted her. We loaded the reluctant winner, struggling and protesting, into the lady's carrier. They left together with Tasha yowling plaintively about this abuse of her person. We wondered if her grumpy, slash-first-ask-questions-later attitude would continue, or if she'd be a different cat again outside the shelter. How far would the lady's patience extend?

At the beginning of November, we had our answer. It was all good news. "I just wanted to let you know that Tasha is adjusting to her new home very well. Oh, sure, there were a few misunderstandings at first (something about not scratching behind a certain ear a certain way). But from the first, she has come to me without much encouragement to rub against my hand and my legs. She is a very sweet little cat and loves to purr while licking your fingers. She loves to sleep on the bed at night and burrow under the covers, and most of the time she follows me wherever I go in my place. She has her independent streak and wants her alone time as well. From what you've told me, she really is a different cat outside the shelter and I am very lucky to have found her."

If anyone was lucky, it was little Tasha. Few people want to adopt an older animal, and even fewer are willing to take a chance that a grumpy old cat will be different in a real home.

The Cat Who Died of a Broken Heart

Sasha was a Katie's Place cat for only a few days. She was a cat who fell through the cracks. Her loss was one of the hardest we ever had to deal with because she did fall through the cracks.

Sasha and Mishka were surrendered to shelter care in July 2005. Midsummer, when kittens stream into shelters by the half dozen, is a bad time for adult cats to need a home, especially those who are plain-looking. Sasha and Mishka were less than three years old, still young, but not young enough compared to litters of cute, eight-week-old babies.

Mishka seemed to have a harder time accepting the loss of their home than her pal who seemed confident and optimistic. Mishka was a lovely cat, a large, long-haired black-and-white. Sasha was plain black. Mishka was timid; at least Sasha, the plainest of the pair, had personality on her side. She was bright, lively, curious, affectionate, and easygoing. With such credentials, at least she had some hope of finding a home. It was faint hope though. There are so many bright, lively, curious, affectionate, easygoing cats in shelter care that many never make it. In summertime, shelters are full to over-flowing. Cages in municipal shelters fill quickly, and some shelters improvise, setting up free-standing cages wherever there's space. Keeping the animals fed and cleaned is as much as they can do.

Sasha and Mishka were closely bonded and shared a cage. While Mishka huddled in their box, Sasha was more receptive to visitors' attention. She leaned into a caress if anyone opened their cage door to pet them. Otherwise, they passed the hot days curled up together. There wasn't much room, and it was comical to see Sasha position herself on top of Mishka and lie with her chin resting on Mishka's head. It may have been crowded for them, but they were happier together than alone.

Weeks turned to months as the summer wore on, and nobody adopted the two cats. They went to a foster home for a while and then came back since there was more chance of finding a home among the many adopters who visit the shelter. No such luck. Sasha greeted visitors hopefully, but her chirrup and expectant face went unnoticed as people's attention was riveted by kittens who gamboled prettily in their cages.

The foster mom advised shelter staff that the cats did not eat much while in her care. A note was posted to watch their intake and output. But when a shelter is busy, it's sometimes hard to track who ate and who eliminated. Their intake and output could have been monitored accurately if they were kept in isolation. But loneliness and loss were already their biggest problems. They at least needed each other. Within a couple of weeks, staff saw that Mishka was jaundiced and sent her to the vet. Sasha still seemed fine. She was active and friendly. She greeted everyone who came by and glowed with pleasure if she got some attention. But soon workers observed that she had not been eating enough either. Cats cannot go without food for long. They become jaundiced and body parts that are usually pink or white will be tinged yellow. It's harder to notice this in a black cat. However, staff eventually noticed that little black Sasha was yellow around the ears and lips even though she still seemed robust and purred when anyone paid attention to her.

Sasha joined Mishka at the vet's where she too received intravenous medications and was coaxed to eat. Mishka began to recover. But nothing seemed to turn the tide for Sasha. She could be persuaded to eat, but she brought it back up. The disease had advanced too far. She grew listless and quiet. No longer did she stand and meow hopefully whenever someone came in. Nothing more could be done. There was no recourse but to put her down. She had become a Katie's Place cat by this point, and the vet gave the final injection as a volunteer stroked her and cradled her head. It was October 2005, four months since their family had left them at a shelter.

Mishka recovered and went to a foster home where she resumed a more normal life. She rallied despite the loss of her lifelong friend as well as her old home. She ate, played, and snuggled with her foster mom who watched her intake like a hawk. In early 2006, she found a new home.

Unwanted pets die every day – by the thousands. It's a tragedy society accepts because the sheer numbers make it seem inevitable. But Sasha's death saddened us because she tried so hard to be noticed. She was only two and a half years old. She was just a plain, black cat who asked everyone she saw for a little attention. Some people gave her a pat and a stroke. Most didn't. There were too many other cats asking for the same thing. So she gave up.

Sasha's faith and hope died long before her body gave out. The tragedy here was the betrayal of her trust. The tragedy is that nobody wanted the love she offered. The tragedy began when she was

Sasha at the vet's on her last day.

born into a world where there are so many cats that they have no value, and it continued when she depended on a home that was gone before she was three years old.

We ached for Sasha particularly among all the animals we'd lost over the years. If poor health took them from us, we could deal with that. We had the comfort of knowing they'd been given every possible chance. But when one dies of what amounts to a broken heart, we have trouble with it.

This story was written for Sasha and for all pets whose love is not returned. Her story was printed in the local paper soon after her death. If it helps save one other pet, then at least some good will have come of her loss.

Bunny Bonds

George and Martha Washington were an unlikely couple. George was a small, solemn, black Dwarf rabbit. Martha was a large, gregarious, ginger-and-white Dutch rabbit. Someone rescued them from an abusive situation, and they lived with their rescuer as house rabbits for several months. Then the rescuer moved and couldn't take them. So in March 2004, they came to us. We couldn't give them the kind of life they'd enjoyed as house rabbits, but they had each other. George and Martha were devoted to each other.

We set them up in a cage upstairs. Once they satisfied their curiosity about their new accommodations, they settled down together in their plastic hut. Martha was the more outgoing of the pair. George was content to follow her lead, but he was equally curious and always peeked from behind her to see what was going on. The hardest part of photographing them was getting them to stay back. They kept coming up to check out the photographer and seemed to consider it a game when she tried to shoo them off. They were amused by everything she did. Finding homes for rabbits is difficult at best, so we moved the pair to a roomy enclosure in the backyard as soon as we could. They enjoyed their life outdoors and were doing well until George developed an abscess in his sinus passages. Because of his fragile condition, they became indoor rabbits again and lived in a cage upstairs. The vet treated George's abscess, but then he developed Snuffles. His medical woes never seemed to end as he wheezed and sneezed, his little black nose constantly crusted and runny. We medicated him daily, and luckily he loved his medicine. All we had to do was hold the dropper, and George would stand on his hind legs to lap from the tip. He often sneezed in fits that lasted a couple of minutes at a time. But as long as he enjoyed life, we were prepared to continue treating his ailments.

Martha was more active than George, yet she never left his side for long. We took them outside on dry days to nibble grass and enjoy the sun in a fenced section of the backyard. The chickens watched them and found them entertaining. George and Martha didn't care about the chickens, they just enjoyed pottering around their little pen and they ignored the birds.

In April 2005, we noticed a bulge around one of George's eyes. The vet discovered a tumour pushing on the back of his eye. It was possible that this was the source of his chronic nasal problems, and we hoped that removing the tumour would cure him. He underwent surgery. Rabbits are delicate creatures so it was risky to even anaesthetize George. The worst case scenario was

174

that he might not survive the operation. However, in his condition, surgery was the best option.

To our relief, it went well. The vet removed the tumour. We had dreaded the possibility of seeing Martha wait in vain for George to return. The vet did say his congestion might not clear up if his problem was a chronic case of Snuffles. We had to watch him for the next while. If the tumour came back, or if his Snuffles didn't abate, it might be time to let the poor fellow go. Breathing was uncomfortable for him and, unlike dogs, rabbits can't breathe through their mouths. Martha would have to cope alone if George's discomfort became too great to continue.

As the days passed, he remained alert and lively. He still loved his medicine, lapping his daily dose greedily. Their visits to the backyard were a joy for them. They played in a plastic tunnel, running through it and popping out the end, to the fascination of the chickens. After a while, we moved them outside again to a sectioned-off area on the north side of the rabbit habitat. That summer, we often saw them resting side by side in a shady corner, leaning against each other. Medicating George outside was no problem since he hurried over for his dropper of strawberry-flavoured liquid. We still had to watch him for the time that

Martha with George

breathing became too difficult.

That time came in August 2005. In one week, George lost a lot of weight and grew listless. His health had been frail for so long, yet he always seemed to rally. He was such a chipper, determined little guy that we wanted to give him every chance. Now he had come as far as he could. Martha spent more and more time on her own. In her animal wisdom, she seemed to recognize that her life with George was ending. George too seemed content by himself, guided by his own instincts. We took him to the vet's for the last time on August 5. Martha carried on placidly, but it was hard seeing her alone in that pen. They had been each other's whole world.

Another bunny, Tom, had arrived at the shelter a month before. Tom was a spunky, white Dwarf with gray points who was found abandoned in an industrial park. Now we put Tom in the pen with Martha and watched to see what would happen. At first, she wanted nothing to do with him. She chased him away when he crept toward her. But Tom was determined to make friends. He inched closer again and touched his nose to hers. She allowed it. Before much longer, they were dining out of the same bowl together, an encouraging sign of good will. Martha was easygoing by nature and she began to accept the persistent little newcomer.

Martha with Tom

After a little while, she allowed him to groom her. He would never be George, but Tom was a likeable fellow – friendly yet respectful.

Over the next month, they settled into a domestic routine. We didn't see the kind of devotion between them that we had seen with Martha and George. But they were comfortable together. We cleaned the habitat extra thoroughly one day, removing all debris, scraping the ground, and putting down new sand and soil. The bunnies thought it was great fun. We turned Martha and Tom's hutch upside down to remove every scrap of debris. Martha clambered up on the tipped-over hutch and enjoyed the novelty of this new perch. Tom delighted in the new digging material; he busied himself investigating that.

We knew Tom liked to dig, but we weren't worried because we had laid wire mesh several inches beneath the ground to prevent the rabbits from digging out. Tom could amuse himself digging all he wanted. They couldn't escape. So we thought, until a volunteer arrived one day to find Tom heading across the parking lot. Apparently he had found the edge of the wire mesh and managed to burrow between that and the fence. There was no visible evidence of a tunnel. But obviously he had completed a tunnel somewhere among their logs, toys and hutch. Martha remained inside the pen. Either she was too big to follow, or she didn't feel inclined to try.

Tom hadn't set out to escape. He just liked digging. He was probably as surprised to reach daylight as we were to see him in the parking lot. Now he had us worried though. If we filled in the gap he'd found in our fortifications, would he find another? The habitat needed to be refortified. However, their main caregiver, Louise, planned to take them home once she completed a habitat in her backyard. Until she was ready, Tom and Martha lived in a spare cage by the front door.

Tom seemed to have grown dependent on Martha. She in turn was surely glad of his company, never having lived alone. But she was more independent. She would stretch out on their sawdust, and Tom would sit beside her with his head buried affectionately in her fur.

A few weeks later, they went to their new home. The last news of the pair came after several months. Little Tom had found himself with a harem since several females occupied the enclosure. He enjoyed being the sole male but was often run over by the females as they zipped around. They all slept together in a corner of their shed on a piece of carpet.

Louise said, "The more I get to know them, the more I love and appreciate the personalities of these wonderful little creatures." Rabbits have their own culture. Discovering their world is a source of delight for those who take the time to learn rabbit lore.

The Cat Who Finally Came In

Porter was a plain, black, homeless cat who was trapped and brought into shelter care. He tested positive for Feline Immunodeficiency Virus (FIV), a legacy of fighting for scarce food and turf with other homeless cats, and he came to live in our Boys' Pen. He was gentle enough, certainly not feral. But he was timid and distrusting. He sat uneasily in our arms and took himself into hiding as soon as we let him go. He was unremarkable in appearance and personality, and with the FIV too, he had virtually no chance of adoption. All we could hope was that he'd settle and be content with us.

It was December 2005 when he arrived, and it was too cold for the cats to spend much time on the porches. But that's where Porter settled himself. For many weeks, he lived out there alone. Each day, we saw his silhouette through the window as he sat in the hanging Papa San chair he'd taken for his bed. He spent his time staring out at the leafless world beyond the wire. Most cats assimilated into shelter life within a couple of weeks. Not Porter. His silhouette on the deserted porch was a lonely sight, and when he still didn't come in after a few more weeks, we made a point of visiting with him.

We had to go out the back door of the barn and past the cleaning area to reach the door of the Boys' Pen porch. People rarely made that trip unless they had to clean or medicate, especially in winter. So Porter was alone most of the time. The expression on his face as he sat in that Papa San chair was bleak. When cats don't welcome human contact, we often see a less-than-enthusiastic expression on their faces at our approach. But Porter didn't care if we came out or not. There was sadness in his expression. It was a look of resignation, as though he believed that any chance of happiness for him was gone. It was a look that cuts you to the quick, and it made us resolve to try coaxing him indoors. We became convinced that his self-imposed exile was not because he preferred to be alone but because he was afraid to come in. He was a plain, lonely soul who needed to be noticed.

By February we were still visiting him out on the porch. He came to the edge of his chair to meet us, and he rubbed and rolled and drooled. When we left, he followed us to the porch door and looked wistful as he watched us walk away. After each visit, we went to the cat door in the Boys' Pen, hoping to lure him inside. But he had always returned to his hanging chair where he sat staring out at the rain. One day a couple of us decided to make him come in. One of us pushed the mildly-panicked Porter through the cat door from the porch while the other waited inside to receive him and hold him.

To Porter, the indoors was as alien as the moon. He stiffened in the volunteer's grasp and whimpered. She cradled him firmly, talking softly to him. That was music to his ears. Before long, he was circling the volunteers' legs on the Boys' Pen floor and thrusting his head into their hands. He made a display of paw flapping and growling if the other cats came too close. But as long as a human was present and soothing him, he was comfortable. When the volunteers left, he slipped back out to the porch.

He was large and solidly built, but he didn't seem to know it. To him, the other cats were lions who could demolish him with a swipe. When we visited the porch, it was such an event in his long, quiet days that he became overstimulated and gave little nips. This was just excitement, but the nips could hurt. He didn't know his own strength.

He joined the world inside the barn by imperceptible degrees. At the end of February, he came inside if a volunteer called to him from the cat door, and he stayed inside when she left. By May he spent as much time inside as out. He didn't want the other cats close enough to touch him, but he learned to relax among them as the weather warmed up and they began spending time on the porch too.

By midsummer, Porter was fully integrated into life at the barn, and we saw in him a vulnerable and deeply loving soul. He would reach into our hands for a caress with such enthusiasm that he nearly fell over, and then he'd roll onto his back, displaying his tummy in a gesture of trust. He no longer gave nips of overexcitement. He still felt uneasy about the other cats who joined him to compete for our attention. He'd try to drive them back with a hiss and a swipe. But they were a thick-skinned bunch, inured to displays of feline ferocity. They ignored him and pursued their own bids for affection.

Within a year of arriving, Porter was the most affectionate cat in the place. His thirst for love told us how painfully lonely he must have been in his homeless days. Those were wretched days when the terrors of other homeless cats competing for survival, and human rejection if he dared seek help, scarred him nearly beyond recovery. It took him many months to relax and trust again. When he did, he made up for lost time. Big and exuberant, Porter knew nothing of subtlety. If you sat down, your lap was fair game. He didn't wait for an invitation.

One day a volunteer sprawled on the Boys' Pen couch, tired from a long day. She stretched out, closed her eyes, and let her body sink, forgetting where she was. Immediately she felt a thud on her chest, and she opened her eyes to find herself looking into Porter's face. He stood with a forepaw on each shoulder and grinned at her in a surge of affection. He was cheerfully unaware that he was imposing. In his heart, he was still just a tiny, black kitten who wanted a cuddle.

Katie's Place felt like home to Porter now. He gave full expression to his playful, kittenish nature in games at the water bowl. He had a peculiar habit of paddling in it. We once saw him just standing with his forepaws immersed to his ankles. He would splash around and make quite a mess. We put up a note to keep the food and water far apart so at least his forays into the water bowl wouldn't leave the kibble sodden. It had mystified us for a long time that chunks of kitty litter were always embedded between his furry toes like cement. We tried chipping it out, a procedure he didn't enjoy. Now we knew how it got there. A damp foot in clay litter creates a cement shoe, and that influenced our later decision to trial pine pellet litter.

Katie's Place and the volunteers were the only home and family Porter would ever have. On April 9, 2007, we lost our boy. He crashed very suddenly, and we took him to the vet's for the last time that morning. He'd been fine as recently as the previous Saturday. The first sign of his decline was when he didn't come to one of his favourite volunteers for his usual lovefest. She went in search of him and found him sleeping in a hidey hole on the porch. It wasn't like Porter to miss a visit, but we all have times when we're too sleepy.

Then the volunteer doing afternoon meds on Sunday noticed that his eyes just "looked sick." He complained when she gave him his meds and cleaned his face. He had developed a mild case of URI and was getting medicine to stave off secondary infections. That day, he seemed to have more than simple URI. He wasn't himself, and if it hadn't been Easter Sunday, the volunteer might have taken him to the vet's right then and there. But she gave it until morning to see if the antirobe would perk him up. Early the next day, the volunteer on morning meds found him flat out and took him straight to the vet's. It didn't matter whether it was liver failure or kidney failure or cancer. The FIV and a hard life had caught up with him. It was time to help him pass.

Porter was special to us. We saw him evolve from a somber recluse to become the most loving cat in the shelter. Once he embraced us as his family, he was one of the first to greet us when we arrived, one of the first to ask for pets, and one of the first to dive into a lap. Often he had the coveted position on a volunteer's chest with his face at her chin while the other cats settled for lap space behind him. He accepted them as friends and snoozed in a pile with them when we weren't around.

He was a common, weather-beaten, black, street cat. He was our Porter. We will cherish the memory of this cat who missed love in his life so much but who made up for lost time in the end.

When Someone Saw Sweetness in a Sour Face

Misty was an older, black-and-white cat who arrived at the shelter under protest. It was February 2005. She was ten years old and came from a home she had loved and where, no doubt, she had been loved. Her elderly person had passed away. This is the most difficult circumstance for a pet. If they lose a home where they weren't wanted, or had no home at all, adjusting is easier. Losing a home where you were loved is hard.

Misty wasn't happy at the shelter, but she enjoyed attention. She seemed grateful for the reassurance of a kind touch, and she was soon curious about this new place. We moved her from her new-cat condo to a communal pen. This was the first time in her life that Misty was among other cats. Everything caught up with her and she snapped. She lit into Goody Sam, tearing his poor ear. We put her in a cage in the communal room. The security of confinement, and separation from the other cats, seemed to soothe her. She was still grumbly but calm.

After a few days, we opened her cage door so she could leave when she was ready. But in Misty's mind, that cage belonged to her now, and there she stayed. She liked to burrow into her blankets. She spent most of her time curled up with her head covered and her hindquarters exposed. It was easier to cope when the bedding blocked the sound, sight, and scent of the shelter. Alone in the dark, she would have felt as close as possible to her old life.

If we rolled the covers back, she enjoyed a few pets and a cheek scratch. Her concern was the other cats. At her age, with a lifetime in a quiet home behind her, she couldn't adjust to living among them. It was a dilemma. Nobody wanted to adopt a grumbly old cat, and Misty would be grumbly as long as she lived among other felines.

One volunteer observed that her appearance didn't help her case. A small, black patch formed a moustache below her nose; the rest of her face was white. Her expression was always stern. "With a face like Hitler, chances are slim that she'll be adopted," the volunteer said. Someone else suggested Charlie Chaplin as a kinder comparison. But Chaplin's face was never as disapproving as Misty's. The volunteer who saw a resemblance to Hitler developed a soft spot for Misty. She campaigned to promote her to Barn Cat. These were cats who, by reason of health or temperament, could not live in the communal rooms, and they had the run of the barn.

There was a limit to the number who could be Barn Cats of course, or the purpose was defeated. When the volunteer who championed her case was on duty, Misty knew she'd get free time in the barn, and she was cheerful and affectionate during those times. The residents of her pen enjoyed the break from her irritability as much as she enjoyed being away from them. She scolded any cat who annoyed her, and if they moved anywhere within three feet of her, that annoyed her. It wasn't a large room. Living with Misty was hard.

As June wore on, Misty's breaks from the communal room became longer and longer. She showed no inclination to leave the upstairs area. She was happy just to wander around the hall and then settle in a corner. Inevitably, she won official Barn Cat status. Our open hours were the only times the common areas became crowded. Misty handled the crowds with forbearance, choosing to withdraw when it became too hectic for her.

The open hours on July 23, 2005 were to be memorable. That was the day someone fell in love with Misty. We didn't expect anyone to notice her. There were too many friendly cats and young cats who gathered around people hoping for attention. Misty preferred to sit apart and watch. It was beneath her to beg for attention. People rarely approached her since her natural facial expression was sullen at best. But one family looked at her and saw beauty. They petted her, and Misty soaked it up. The people and the cat connected. This was the kind of moment we live for. We look at some of our residents who are short on natural charm, and we hope the moment will come when a visitor sees the loving soul behind fierce or frightened eyes.

The family beamed with pleasure as we loaded Misty into a carrier to go home. "She's a nice cat," they said with feeling as her strident protests at being confined rose from the carrier. The dour old girl had found her match. They set off, the proud family and their new pet, Misty's howls growing fainter as they disappeared.

The connection they felt never faded. We heard from them later in a note that said, "She fit in from the first day and never a problem. She is so much company. I talk to her all the time and she answers with a meow and rolls on her back."

Below the note was a photo of Misty sprawled in a sun spot on the rug, all fours in the air, peering at the camera through her forepaws. Her expression was almost sweet.

From Devil to Angel

Carmen was a dainty young tabby. She came to us in September 2005 from a vet's office which sometimes had cats to adopt. She could no longer stay there because she suddenly became impossible. We discovered what they meant when we met her. If anyone came too close, she let out a bloodcurdling shriek. In fact, you really didn't have to get close. She let out a shriek if anyone passed by or looked at her. At the shelter, we covered her new-cat cage. It was the only way to get any peace. Once we heard bumping noises from inside, and when we peeped under the cover, we saw that she was playing. But the face peeping at her elicited another hair-raising screech. Everyone – human and feline – quickly learned to leave Carmen alone.

As time passed, she improved a bit. We let her out in the Main Pen, but she stayed close to her new-cat cage where she felt safe. She was uneasy in the open area. When we put a new cat into her old cage, Carmen was beside herself. She spent a whole day complaining and pacing back and forth in front of the cage, glaring at its

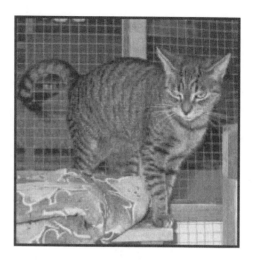

hapless occupant. In the end, she contented herself with a basket.

     She wasn't mean or dangerous. She was just loud. She'd swat at you if you came too close, but she swatted defensively, she didn't attack. Carmen's dark secret was that she was scared of everybody. Somehow she learned that screaming made everyone back off. The fiercer the scream, the faster everyone backed away. So Carmen perfected her shriek. We weren't sure what we'd do with her. Obviously, adoption was out of the question. Her shrieks reverberated around the shelter continuously at first while we pondered the dilemma. But they began to grow less frequent. So maybe there was hope that she'd settle down. Until she did, we explained to startled visitors, "Oh that's Carmen...." Life at a shelter is what it is.

     She caught a cold within a few weeks of arriving, and that knocked the scream right out of her. When we found her sleeping on the couch one day, she let us stroke her as much as we wanted. That scared us. No unholy shrieks, no piercing screams – this just wasn't right. So she went to the vet's for a couple of days. She still wasn't back in shrieking form when she returned,

and we put her in a cage where we could give her medicated food and be assured that she was the one eating it.
She began to recover. Soon the medicating volunteers were syringing her meds into her mouth. She was
getting feisty again, but she could be handled. By the
time she had almost recovered, she'd hurry over for
attention when we arrived, and she'd nuzzle for a couple
of seconds before deciding that our presence was an
unsolicited invasion of her space. Then she'd lash out in
a disorganized fashion. But she didn't shriek anymore.
Perhaps the Carmen Scream was a thing of the past.
Now if she could just get over her hypersensitivity to
attention....

Carmen enjoyed having her own private suite while
she was sick. When her health returned, she was no
longer a submissive little cat. She was the old testy
Carmen. The time came to reintegrate her into the population of the Main Pen. She couldn't live in the cage at
the top of the stairs forever. Even if she liked it, we
needed it for other cats. But who would have the honour
of moving Carmen to the Main Pen? This delicate task
was avoided by all the volunteers for a while. One day,
the move was quickly accomplished by Evelyn, who had
gone head to head with recalcitrant cats before.

Some screeches from the Main Pen were the first
indication to some of us that Carmen had returned. We
rushed over, fearing a murder was in progress, and noticed Carmen skulking around. She found she was at
square one with the other cats, and she had to reinstill
proper respect in them again. So she screeched with

renewed vigour to remind them all that she was to be given wide berth.

After a long, loud week or two, she settled down again. From a hidey hole atop a perch that she claimed as her own, she only squawked if her space was invaded. She greeted us warmly. But when she reached her limit for stimulation, she still lashed out, complaining and flapping at the person she had nuzzled a moment before.

In January 2006, the impossible happened. Carmen got herself adopted. We never listed her for adoption because she was too high-strung. We couldn't even find homes for all our sweet-tempered animals. But Carmen had begun to mellow. We no longer heard any hair-raising shrieks, and she asked for attention more and more frequently. Whenever we entered the Main Pen, the most sociable cats gathered and wove around us joyfully. We had to acknowledge each one, stroking every back and scritching every cheek that passed under our hands. One day a volunteer noticed it was Carmen's cheek under her hand. Carmen was beginning to blend in.

A man came during our open hours one Sunday to look for a pet, and Carmen was among the cats working the crowd that day. He described his former cat who died, and she sounded as high-strung as Carmen. While he handled her, Carmen reached the limit of her very limited tolerance and expressed her annoyance pointedly. He was unfazed. He said he'd like to bring his daughter to meet her. Even as we nodded, we were sure we wouldn't see him again. But he did come back, and his daughter was as taken with Carmen as he was. They ended up adopting her (after which we threw out the book, *Identifying Unadoptable Cats*). Carmen would be their one cat which would suit her just fine. We wish only good things for people to whom frenzied swatting and squawking is endearing behaviour.

A couple of weeks later the man phoned us. We felt a moment of apprehension when the caller identified himself as Carmen's adopter. Had she worn out her welcome? She hadn't. In fact, it seemed that the demonic little twerp had turned into a sweet angel.

We try to tell adopters that the animal they see in a shelter will be different (and even better) in a real home. In Carmen's case, we never expected so dramatic a change. She was a perfect example of the profound influence of environment. You can't judge a book by its cover, and you can't judge it from the shelf it's sitting on either.

A Fur Rug With Asthma

"Mic" stands for Mistaken Identity Cat. He was a
laid-back fellow with long, tabby-and-white fur who
came to us in June 2004. Staff at another shelter called to
say they had a cat that was tattooed to us. It turned out he
wasn't one of ours, but when his home could not be
located he stayed. Making himself comfortable, he spent
most of his time sprawled on his back with his paws
flung out. He was so handsome and easygoing that he
was soon adopted. But they returned him just as quickly
due to litter pan problems. We had him checked by our
vet and learned that he'd developed a bowel sensitivity
which required a special diet.

The only way Mic could get his special diet was to
live apart from the other cats, so we promoted him to
Barn Cat, coveted status which confers on the bearer
access to the common areas of the barn. His bowel sensitivity eventually cleared up but he kept his Barn Cat
status. He was also diagnosed with asthma and needed
prednisone daily. His odds of adoption dropped because

of his asthma, so we decided if he was going to be with us for a long time, he might as well stay a Barn Cat. The one problem we had with him as a Barn Cat was his careless habit of snoozing in high-traffic areas. Where Mic had been inclined to sprawl full-length in the middle of his communal room, he now sprawled full-length in the middle of the common areas. Once or twice he was stepped on which provoked a yelp and an aggrieved look. But the experience didn't teach him to stay out of the way. Mic continued to lounge in the middle of the floor, the image of lazy comfort. He was as content as a cat could be, snoozing most of the day, spread-eagled like a small fur rug. He ignored the bustle of volunteers working around him. Nothing ever seemed to upset him.

The daily prednisone controlled his asthma, but it was increasing his girth and he began to look as though he'd swallowed a watermelon. So we talked to the vet about what else we could do. The only other option was an asthma puffer. We decided to try it using a mask adapted for a feline face. Mic didn't like it at first. But he soon allowed us to put the mask over his nose without so much as twitching a whisker, and he began to recover a more normal shape.

For a supremely laid-back cat, he had quite a determined streak. When the next summer rolled around, Mic took to spending time outside. At first he was content to lounge close by. Then he began wandering farther afield. When we

noticed him trotting down the driveway we herded him back. He was surprisingly fast for a portly cat, but we worried he wouldn't be fast enough to escape a predator. So we locked him in the barn when we weren't available to supervise him.

The one remaining exit was a dog door used by Max, the German Shepherd who belonged to the barn's owners and who chose to spend his time at the barn. Mic couldn't use that door, guarded as it was by an excitable German Shepherd, so we thought. However, when Mic found himself locked in, he eyed Max's door and decided that what worked for a dog should work for a cat. He climbed the gate separating Max's area, nonchalantly ignoring the dog who should have served as a deterrent.

Unfortunately Max considered him a trespasser. They duked it out, the hairy little cat and the goofy but annoyed German Shepherd. Horrified, we tossed Mic into Solitary to think about his reckless behaviour. We couldn't keep him confined though. He'd had free run of the shelter for too long. He was unhurt by his encounter with Max, and as autumn brought cooler weather, he was choosing to spend his time sprawled on the floor again anyway. We reinstated his Barn Cat privileges.

Mic came close to being adopted a couple of times. His amiable personality won people over, but each person seemed to be put off by his asthma. So his daily routine of posing a trip hazard continued uninterrupted. He was roused to action only by sounds of distress. Mic had appointed himself keeper of the peace and guardian of us all, feline or human.

The volunteers were medicating a feral cat one day. The cat in question had no wish to be held, never mind medicated, and she protested as though it were a lethal assault. Mic heard her shrieks and, convinced we were murdering a cat, he leapt to her aid, boxing the volunteers soundly on the legs. He settled down quickly once he realized it was a false alarm. But the look on his usually-placid face conveyed his opinion that the volunteers and cat were irresponsible and the whole episode had been a needless waste of energy.

On another day, a volunteer was closing up and checked the placement of the heater. She nudged it with her foot, not noticing Katie on the other side. Katie had lived in the barn since before we arrived and was an ill-tempered cat who resented our presence. Cranky Katie swiped at the foot, catching the ankle with her claws, and the volunteer yelped. Mic had been sleeping near by. As soon as the volunteer yelped, he sprang from his bed and stood poised near the spot Katie had occupied barely a moment before. Katie had jumped back when Mic leapt, and she stood defensively against the wall, still complaining. It was over within seconds; they both relaxed and turned away. Mic would tolerate being medicated and stepped on. He would tolerate being taken to our community presentations where he was handled by crowds of people. Mic would tolerate many irritations. But he would not tolerate abuses of his cats and people.

At the end of January 2006, we held a special open house to mark our sixth anniversary. Mic abandoned his spot in the middle of the floor when visitors streamed in and he lounged in an armchair by the door, allowing everyone to admire him. One man gave him a thorough, luxurious brushing, and Mic relaxed into it. You could almost see a dreamy smile on his face. There was clearly some bonding going on between the two. The man and his family were frequent visitors and had taken a real liking to Mic. That day, they took the plunge and decided to adopt him, asthma and all.

We knew we would miss him, but we were happy for him. Now Mic would have just one family to look after rather than a whole shelter full of animals and volunteers. He would have less to worry about – in so far as he ever worried about anything.

The Ultimately Unexcitable Cat

Pancake and her siblings were born in a supermarket warehouse. The staff was unaware of their existence. They discovered the cat and kittens one day when they moved some boxes and exposed their hiding place. The little creatures scattered in all directions, but they managed to round them up and bring them to Katie's Place. It was the spring of 2003.

The babies were on the cusp of becoming feral. They had never seen a human up close, and they were not happy about being handled. So they went into foster care for socializing. Within a couple of months, Pancake's two siblings were adopted. Even their mother was adopted after a few months. But Pancake's foster mom could offer no more time to the skittish youngster. Between her job, family and volunteer shift, her hands were full.

So Pancake came to the shelter where we hoped she would catch an adopter's eye. Unfortunately she was an ordinary black-and-white cat who hadn't learned to court human attention. She preferred feline company. The

volunteers couldn't give her the attention she needed to
become a lap cat. Weeks turned to months, and she found
family in the cats with whom she lived, choosing more
and more to slip into a cubby hole while people were
around.

She made some close feline friends. One shy, orange
tabby named Guinness had a terminal heart condition
and rarely moved. Pancake was often seen curled up
beside him until the day he died a year later. Then we
saw her mostly with another black-and-white cat, Sharla,
who shared her opinion of humans. When Sharla was
adopted, Pancake carried on unconcerned. She might
never have a home herself, and that would be fine with
her. She considered potential adopters an intrusion. For
their part, adopters passed over the plain-looking cat
who watched them skeptically from the sidelines. She
had grown up to be a phlegmatic little creature who
watched activities without reaction.

As she got older she became portly from inactivity.
We saw her play a few spirited games with a ball in a
circular tube. But this burst of activity was not enough to
keep her trim. So she was prone to a chubby cat's complaint, matted fur on her lower back where she couldn't
reach to groom. To our surprise, she allowed us to remove the mats, brush her and even give her a pedicure.

Some days, she lay placidly and allowed us to stroke
her. Other days, she'd slip away. It depended on her
mood. We concluded that Pancake was not so much
learning to enjoy human contact as she was disinclined
to escape it. If you touched her, she flinched with surprise. But running away took effort. So she accepted the

touch while her face betrayed the debate. "Do I lie here and take it, or do I get up and move?" Some days, it was easier to take it. We found her snoozing on a shelf one day and gave her a stroke. With other cats,

that was enough to make them lift their heads. But Pancake didn't respond. We stroked her more firmly. Nothing. We shook a limp paw. Her breathing was the only sign of life. However, in the dim light of her hiding place, we saw one eye peering at us reproachfully. If she could speak, her single word would have been "What?" Eventually she did lift her head and regard us aggrievedly with both eyes for a moment. Then she curled up tight, putting an end to the exchange. If anyone was looking for a paper weight or bookend, we could have recommended Pancake. She was as inert as the food for which she'd been prophetically named.

Pancake's chances of being adopted were slim to none. But was life good for her? She didn't seem unhappy. She didn't seem happy. Pancake was just Pancake. She deserved more, and one of us in particular felt for her. In March 2006, a volunteer took her home after more than two and a half years at the shelter. She would have the company of other feline misfits the volunteer had adopted.

To everyone's delight, she blossomed, venturing more and more out of her shell into her new world. She adapted well to the other cats in the house and developed a liking for a battle-scarred old fellow named Gus. She loved being brushed and petted. With every stroke of the brush, she flopped onto her left side, then onto her right side, her purrs growing louder with each touch. When her person spoke to her, she blinked slowly and deliberately, taking in the words, happy to be the object of attention.

Pancake had been content in her years at the shelter, but in a proper home with a family of her own, she became an animated, responsive cat. She shed the old identity of Pancake, and she was called Samantha from that time on.

The Cat Who Conquered His Clothing

Cosmo was left at the municipal shelter in September 2004. His family cited a new baby as the reason for giving him up. He was a sensitive cat. He tended to be introverted, and he avoided strangers. So needless to say, the busy municipal shelter, with animals and people coming and going, didn't put him at ease. When he became difficult, he came to Katie's Place where he settled in although he wasn't too happy about living with other cats. It left him short-tempered, and potential adopters were put off when he rejected their attention. On quiet days, he came to us asking for pets. He seemed to smile if we gave him a few strokes. However, living in a shelter didn't bring out the best in him. He also needed a diet that prevents urine crystals. It was a minor demand, but it was one more obstacle toward finding him a home.

He was a long-haired, black-and-white cat with pink ears that looked as though they didn't belong on his black head. Mats formed in his long fur and we'd try to brush him. But he squirmed like a fidgety child and never allowed us to finish. So we ended up shaving him. Underneath all that fur, Cosmo was a rotund little fellow. He made a comical picture, shaved to the skin and left with a lion's mane, booties, a tuft on his tail, and a droopy undercarriage.

When Mic was adopted, it created an opening for a new Barn Cat to live in the common areas away from other cats. Cosmo seemed the best choice since he'd been with us for a while with no prospects for adoption. He assumed his new position with delight and spent his time pottering around – upstairs, downstairs, and back upstairs again. He liked to see who was arriving when he heard the door open. One volunteer said she saw a personality change within a few days of him leaving the communal room. He was mellower and more inclined to enjoy a fuss.

By February, he had become so matted again that it must have been uncomfortable. The weather was bitingly cold, and the heating in the barn wasn't the best. But he needed shaving, and he could wear a sweater, at least until the weather warmed up. Cosmo had other ideas. Even while groggy from sedation, he refused to let us dress him. He wandered around with bare skin exposed to the cold. When two volunteers were free, we tried again to put his sweater on. Again, he resisted. Then we worried that even if we succeeded, he might snag his claws in the loosely-knit sweater and become entangled. So one of us went to find safer attire, something easy to put on him.

The volunteer returned with a fleece-lined dog coat. This time, we succeeded in dressing him.
Cosmo was furious. He sat glowering and held himself as rigid as a brick in the new coat. While we watched, he began to list like a sinking ship until he toppled over sideways, still stiff as a brick. We set the rigid little figure upright on the floor. He began to walk, moving only his feet from the ankles down. Looking like a strange, mechanical toy, he toddled a few steps and flopped over. Then all four legs began working while he grumbled in a hum like a large, angry bee.

As we watched, he wriggled his paws inside of the coat and pushed upwards against it from inside. The other cats stared from their pens, transfixed with amazement. All eyes in the room were riveted to Cosmo. Then his head disappeared inside the coat and, in one movement, he thrust it off, popping out backwards, and strolled away leaving it crumpled on the floor. It was a performance worthy of Houdini. We admitted defeat. After that, we left Cosmo's bed beside the heater. If he chose to wander into colder areas, he was on his own.

When we weren't trying to brush him or dress him, he was good-natured enough. Being a Barn Cat agreed with him. Sometimes he patrolled the shelter, peering into different pens as though doing a bed check. He

didn't try to get outside. He didn't even spend much time
downstairs. The red sweater that we had tried to put on
him lay in his bed in the upstairs hall. He slept with it
like his special blankie and kneaded it with a smile in his
eyes. Maybe it was a symbol of his victory.

One day he was outraged to find Shamus sleeping in
his bed on his sweater. Shamus never backed down in a
confrontation, so Cosmo didn't know what to do. He
tried to content himself with Shamus's bed. But it wasn't
the same. He circled his own bed, glaring at Shamus.
Shamus ignored him. He sat down as close as he could,
applying the pressure of proximity. Shamus didn't care.
Cosmo obviously felt that his behaviour was vile. He
looked at us as though hoping we'd do something. The
day was saved when a volunteer began dishing out soft
food which Shamus considered more rewarding than
lying in Cosmo's bed. Once the trespasser had removed
himself, Cosmo sniffed the bed pointedly. Satisfied that
Shamus hadn't contaminated it, he climbed in and settled
down, glowing with satisfaction. Order was restored in
his world.

By August 2006, he had been in shelter care for
nearly two years. He was a self-willed little cat who
liked things a certain way. Random pats from passing
visitors did not align with his expectations, and he could
be peevish when things weren't as he expected. During
our open hours, we introduced people to other cats and
left him alone.

When a young couple came during open hours on
August 13 and said they wanted to adopt Cosmo, each
volunteer in turn exclaimed, "Cosmo?" believing they

must have heard wrong. The people had read about him and his eccentricities on the web. They met him, they liked him, and the formalities were completed. Cosmo had a home. But we had to send him off without his sweater. It seemed that some misguided volunteer had removed the grubby, tattered sweater from his bed for washing, and we couldn't find it.

Within a few days, we received an update from his new home. We had worried about how he'd handle the adjustment after being with us for so long. Sometimes we have to fight the crazy feeling that we're betraying them by sending them away. The news was good. His family reported that he purred a lot and had allowed them to brush him a bit. "He's a really cuddly, friendly kitty," his new person wrote, "and I've noticed that he loves his chin being scratched. Today he let me give him a big hug, and he was purring so much he was drooling." We read the note again and looked at each other. Were they talking about Cosmo?

Several months later, we received another update. "Cozzie has grown trusting and he is comfortable with me cutting his fur balls out. He even enjoys his daily brushings." It seems that Cosmo's new home met with his expectations of a well-ordered world. He didn't really ask much. All he wanted was a dependable home and a family that felt no urge to dress him.

A Cat Who Couldn't Keep His Balance

Willy Wonka was first seen in October 2005 when he staggered through someone's backyard. A cat lover looked out her window and was shocked to see this black cat stumbling and weaving across her property. Although there was no sign of injury, he could barely stand. She rushed him to the vet's, and while they worked over him she contacted Katie's Place. The vet found no sign of poisoning, no illness and no injury. They did a variety of diagnostics while Willy enjoyed a hearty meal and reveled in all the attention. He seemed less concerned about his plight than were any of the people trying to help him. Although he clearly had neurological problems, he was a calm, friendly, happy cat.

After all the diagnostics were completed, the only thing we knew for sure was that Willy was uncoordinated, yet healthy in every other regard. He was a neutered male, less than five years old, with an unreadable tattoo and no microchip. His finder put up posters, and the municipal shelter was notified.

His problem was narrowed down to Cerebellar Hypoplasia, a neurological condition that causes loss of motor control. Willy would have been born with this condition if his mother contracted an infection while pregnant. But why such a vulnerable cat was outside is a mystery. He could not have survived for long among dangers such as predators and traffic. He was a trusting, lovable fellow. Why wasn't anyone looking for him? Everything possible was done to reunite him with his home to no avail. He came to Katie's Place.

He could walk and do everything cats do. He rubbed his cheek against a wall, slipped to the floor and got up to continue rubbing. His one problem was poor coordination. That, and being a plain, black cat would make it hard to find him a home.

Willy settled in and was soon lurching nonchalantly around a communal room. Though he was plain looking and ungainly, he had enough charm to make up for any deficits. If we called him, he tumbled from his favourite cubby hole and made his way over, hoping for a cuddle. He'd nuzzle, slide to the floor and pick himself up to carry on. If we cuddled him, he leaned into us and pressed his head into our hands with heartfelt tenderness. When the visit ended, he clambered back into his cubby hole.

The other cats in his room were sometimes unnerved by his inexplicable movements. It caused Willy a few social problems. Occasionally, we heard him scuffle with some other cat who was no doubt agitated by his lurching nearby them. But he never showed any scratches or battle scars. Either he was more adept than he appeared, or the other cats held back, knowing he was no real threat. Still, he spent most of the time in his chosen cubby hole. Poor fellow. It might have been the single place he felt safe. When we were in the room, he'd always come out and wobble around, cheerfully rubbing and schmoozing.

He was vulnerable and he knew it. That was the only sense in which his disability troubled him. Otherwise, he probably didn't feel any different from any other cat. One time, he turned when he heard us call his name and immediately fell over a scratching post. He didn't chafe or fret. Instead, he took advantage of the post to sharpen his claws before continuing his journey toward us.

Another time, a volunteer dropped by the shelter when everyone had finished and gone. Most of the cats were snoozing. But loud meows wafted downstairs, calling to her. It was Willy, standing at the wire of his pen by the stairwell. He pushed his head against the wire for a head scratch and sharpened his claws in exultant greeting. He fell over twice and got up without a second thought.

We had hoped to find a foster home for Willy since he was never at ease among the other cats. It's hard enough to find foster homes for normal cats; finding one for a spastic cat was going to be a challenge. The volunteers knew Willy was a completely capable, lovable little guy. One volunteer had lost her cat to cancer not long ago. As painful as this loss was, it created an opportunity.

On January 7, 2006, the volunteer arrived, very excited, to take Willy home. She showed us the bed she'd bought for him and his new collar and toys. They went home together that day, Willy trusting and obliging as ever about heading off to a new place. The volunteer later chided that he was a vocal cat who demanded attention. But she indulged him willingly. She couldn't hide that she doted on him and was proud to be his person.

The Cat Who Was a Hopeless Case

When Denton arrived at the end of April 2006, we didn't know if this cat had any future. He came from a place with too many cats, numbering in the dozens, and he suffered from neglect. Most of the cats from this place were reasonably healthy, but Denton was dirty, sick and unresponsive. He had ongoing diarrhea, and it seemed he'd become so depleted and dirty that he gave up trying to clean himself. His medium-length fur was caked with dried diarrhea, giving him a distinct aroma. He was also badly matted along his flanks. We had to wonder how long he'd been that way and if he had any hope of recovery.

The vet gave him a full exam and treated his diarrhea. There was hope. We also had his mats shaved off, which helped clean him up a bit. It didn't improve his appearance though. Only his flanks needed shaving so he was left bald on both sides with a Mohawk down his back and a tuft at the end of his tail. He was thin, and when viewed from the front, he was ridiculously narrow. An upper respiratory infection complicated his woes. His

face had
crusted
over as
his nose
dripped
and his
eyes
watered.
If his
third

eyelids hadn't covered so much of his eyes due to poor health, you might have noticed that he was also cross-eyed. There would be no beauty contest prizes for this cat.

An appealing personality would have redeemed the appalling image he presented. But he sat hunched in his bed, silent and unresponsive. A few optimistic volunteers dedicated themselves to drawing him out. They sat by his new-cat cage, stroking him and talking to him. For several weeks, we saw little response. He seemed resigned, almost as though he was waiting for us to discover that we were not stroking a pretty cat and walk away. But the volunteers persisted, and gradually he began to come out of his shell. We told him he was a handsome boy, lying through our teeth, and he reached into our caresses as he grew more confident that we were his friends. He still never made a sound, but he rolled from one bald flank to the other as he gave himself up to the pleasure of feeling loved.

Imperceptibly, his health returned. His fur became clean and soft (where he had fur). His third eyelids went down, and his phlegmatic little face regarded us with a new brightness in his eyes. Now when we opened his cage door, he looked up with trusting, happy expectation and began purring right away. He turned out to be a gentle-natured, loving soul.

It looked like Denton could enjoy a normal life among the other cats, so we put him in the Main Pen. We expected at best that he would settle comfortably and enjoy attention when we sought him out. He was still a self-effacing creature despite his increased confidence. He surprised us though with a complete change in behaviour. We'd arrive to see him dancing around the floor, tossing a toy in the air and scampering after it. He greeted us and chatted nonstop in his high voice. He was still homely with his crossed eyes and Mohawk haircut. But he became one of the most cheerful, affectionate characters at the shelter.

When anyone went into the Main Pen, Denton followed them around so eagerly that he didn't notice whose space he might be invading when he hopped from perch to perch, keeping up with the visitor. Other cats gave him an icy stare as his tail flicked them in the face. Denton was happily oblivious. He became a favourite with all the volunteers.

It was inevitable that such an endearing cat would attract adopters' notice despite being plain with an odd haircut. When visitors dropped in, Denton was one of the first to greet them, offering his own version of adoring fanfare. In July 2006, he was adopted. It was the middle of the slowest season for adoptions. He found a home before many attractive cats who had been there much longer. We never would have predicted this for the sick, withdrawn cat who looked so repulsive only ten weeks before. Faith and hope despite hopelessness had paid off again.

A Normal Cat With Odd Homes

We had one case of an animal who was remarkable not so much for herself as for the people in her life. Lacey, a white cat, came to us in September 2005. She was a senior and she arrived in the arms of her person, a tall, gruff, older man. He thrust the cat at us and said she was dying so we had to take her. We looked from the cat to the man and back to the cat again. She was clear eyed and curious with a soft, clean coat. We looked at her more critically. She seemed perfectly healthy. We tried to get more information from him and tried making suggestions to help keep them together, all to no avail. He had decided she was dying and he was done with her. By now we were reluctant to see the poor animal go back to such a peculiar home, so we took her. That was the last we ever saw of the man.

Lacey was almost as gruff as her former person. Finding herself in a shelter was upsetting, and she seemed to suspect it was all our fault. We had to be cautious when cleaning her new-cat cage. But she soon began to mellow. Within a couple of weeks, she decided that we were her friends, and she greeted us with eager meows and begged for attention. She was a bright, spirited, affectionate girl although she could be bossy with the other cats. Cuddling with people was what she loved more than anything else in the world. She climbed into our arms at the first opportunity and would probably have stayed there all day if we'd let her. One thing she was not was "dying."

Lacey couldn't get enough one-on-one attention at the shelter. Older cats are passed over by adopters time and again, even cats like Lacey who called as sweetly as she could, reaching her paw out and looking adoringly at anyone who gave her a pat. Because she was irritable with the other cats, she lived in a single-cat condo. It was hard to see her waiting, day after day, for a few moments of attention, hoping to catch somebody's eye as people walked by. There had to be more to life for Lacey than living by herself at the shelter.

One afternoon during our open hours, a lady walked around meeting all the cats. She seemed moved by them, and she told us she wanted to give a home to the neediest one. Every once in a while, we meet someone like this, and we live for these moments. When people are focused more on giving love than on getting it, they inevitably reap rewards for their patience when their hopeless-case adoption becomes cheerful, trusting and loving.

We always have animals in urgent need of a proper home environment. The hard part is narrowing the list down. The lady seemed inclined to take a pair of senior cats, but she also looked at Lacey. It's harder to find homes for pairs of cats. Yet Lacey was so lonesome. In the end, Lacey won the home. We congratulated ourselves on an exceptional adoption and tried to make it up to Sly and Thumbelina, the senior pair who lost out.

A few weeks later, we were surprised to see the lady return and bring Lacey back. She told us she couldn't keep the little cat because she couldn't give her enough time. We tried to put her mind at rest, saying that Lacey was getting more time with her than she would get at the shelter, and that chances for another adoption were slim for her. But the lady was adamant. She turned Lacey over to us and left. We were dumbfounded since the adopter had been so intent on finding the neediest cat. We've met several people over the years who ask for the cat most needing a home without having expectations of the animal. Never had anyone returned the cat to the shelter they so urgently needed to escape. It was a learning experience for us about misconceptions and misunderstandings.

Ending up at the shelter again was hard on Lacey. She reverted to the unhappy cat we first met, only she seemed more sad than angry this time. Strange relationships with the human species plagued this animal's life. Her predicament tore at our hearts. With many other cats crying for attention, Lacey didn't get the companionship she hungered for. She sat at the front of her cage and called to people in soft, hopeful chirps. If the volunteers were too busy to respond, she returned to her nest in resignation. Her loneliness was palpable. So we broke down and added her to the ranks of Barn Cats who lived in the common areas. She couldn't live in a cage forever, and she couldn't live happily with other cats. We opened her door, and before too long she ventured out and was peeking into the communal rooms. Eventually she chose a shelf as her perch, and we placed her bed there. At least she wasn't isolated anymore.

Within a couple of months, Lacey had explored the entire shelter and found a location that suited her even better than her shelf in the upper hall. She claimed the top of the file cabinet by the main entrance as her home base. She was the first cat people saw when they arrived and the last one they saw when they left. She never tried to get outside. She just enjoyed being the Greeter. For a sociable cat like Lacey, it was ideal. Everyone gave her pets as they came and went.

In June 2006, a former adopter dropped by to say hello. Of course, she met Lacey at her post greeting everyone. We told her about the old girl as she nuzzled her visitor blissfully. The lady's heart went out to her, and by the end of the visit she had decided to adopt her. This lady was devoted to her animals, and we knew it to be an exceptionally good home. Lacey's luck had changed at last. It was all she deserved after her odd experiences with the people in her life.

The Cat Who Went on a "Mad Tear"

Peony, a ten-year-old calico with a thyroid condition, lost her home in June 2006 when her people moved. They tried hard to find a home for her, and she was a well-behaved, affectionate cat. But they learned, as we have, that it's nearly impossible to rehome older cats who need daily medications. When time ran out, they brought her to Katie's Place.

It was a shock for a coddled, older cat to find herself alone in a shelter full of strangers. Peony lay as far back as she could in the carrier she used as a bed and wouldn't come out. We needed to be sure she was eating and drinking before we could release her from the new-cat cage. We saw her drink. She had a funny habit of standing with one paw in her water bowl while she drank. But she needed coaxing to eat. She enjoyed socializing with people but harboured deep suspicions about the other cats. We could only hope that being pretty, good-natured and declawed would make her appealing to adopters despite her age and her need for meds.

She did not adjust well and stayed in the new-cat cage for quite a while. By mid-November, we left her cage door open. She couldn't live there forever. Still she preferred to stay in 'her' cage. Eventually we needed it for a new cat, so Peony claimed a nest in a dark corner of the communal room, and there she stayed. We put food and water at the entrance of her nest. However, other cats could wander by and snack on her meal. We've had the occasional case of cats, usually older, who were so devastated to lose their homes that they stopped eating and could not be coaxed to eat before succumbing to Fatty Liver Syndrome, a fatal consequence of fasting for cats.

Peony was losing weight, so a volunteer took her home where she could be monitored better and get more one-on-one time. A week after moving to her foster home, the old cat was still going downhill. She was getting subcutaneous fluids for dehydration. She had also begun throwing up. The vet gave her an anti-vomiting injection. Within the next couple of hours, she threw up twice more. The outlook for her was grim.

Then in mid-December, the improbable news came that someone wanted to adopt her, problems and all. It was a heaven-sent opportunity. But we had to make sure she was stable before subjecting her to another change of environment. She was thin but had started eating again, and if she maintained her progress, she could tolerate a move within a couple of weeks. All we had to do now was hope the person wouldn't have a change of heart or find a cat elsewhere.

All went well, and Peony was adopted on Christmas Eve, 2006. It was a case of a caring person giving a gift to a fragile, old cat instead of giving herself the most appealing and easiest pet.

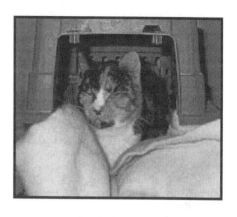

We hoped Peony wouldn't react to the latest change in her life with another downward spiral. If luck was on our side, she'd continue eating and enjoy the peaceful, contemplative life that is the luxury of senior cats with homes.

Two months later, we had an update. The fact that two months passed without dire news was already encouraging. What the note revealed about Peony amazed us.

"The timid, withdrawn little waif with hardly an appetite has now had some time to adjust to her new surroundings and express her true personality," her person wrote. "This darling girl is actually an assertive, determined and persistent little chowhound. And we love her for it.

Our eighteen-year-old cat, Sam, was lonely and we wanted him to have a companion, a quiet, gentle companion. Well, Peony has turned out to be a mighty force. Sam is a loving, mellow cat and we cherish him, but something was missing – call it the exasperation factor. Now we have it in spades.

Kitty meal prep is an experience with Peony constantly meowing and chirruping, urging me to go faster,
and alternating between trying to help by standing on her
hind legs or clamping her front paws around one of my
ankles. As you might imagine, she has gained weight and
developed greater strength and energy, so much so that
she has become quite the accomplished jumper and a
mealtime table surfer if you're not vigilant.

One night, we were putting the finishing touches on
a pasta dinner at the stove when we turned to discover
her in the middle of the dining room table, removing
baguette slices from a plate and lining them up in a row.
It was too funny, but needless to say, all food now remains on the kitchen counters until we're ready to sit
down. When we do settle in to eat, she's right there by
our side. Sometimes she'll stand on her tiptoes and rest
her chin on the edge of the table like a little periscope,
looking for anything that might be within reach of an
outstretched paw. And dessert or snacks on the sofa,
well, that's a recreational event for all of us.

She went on her first mad tear the other night. I
heard the scramble of little cat feet on the tile in the
kitchen, and the next thing I see is Peony roaring across
the living room. When I ran into the kitchen to find out
what caused this, I found one of her little squishy balls
still rolling along the floor. A wild game of chase the ball
followed as she waited for me again and again to throw
it her way. Those little paws pack a wallop; Peony has an
awesome overhand smash!"

The letter made our eyes widen. "Mad tear?"
"Mealtime table surfer?" Peony? We could hardly be-

lieve that this introverted senior had become a mischievous imp. Our fear had been that her adopter would be
unable to deal with such a withdrawn old cat. She was
just lucky that they were able to deal with the outrageous
antics of a cat whose true nature we never guessed.

The Feral Cat Who Became a Social Butterfly

The first thing that struck us about Xerox was his appearance. He was one of the most beautiful cats we'd ever seen. His slender build, his perfect Spotted Tabby markings, his silver colouring, his well-proportioned face – elegant! He was delicate and he moved with fluid grace. The second remarkable thing about him was that he came to us as a feral cat who grew up without human contact. A true feral would never willingly accept human touch. Yet, as we were to learn, Xerox would not only accept it, he would welcome it.

He was trapped as a young adult and turned over to the municipal shelter in November 2005. As a feral, they transferred him to Katie's Place. We keep ferals at the shelter until we're certain they are feral and not just long-term homeless pets who can regain trust with time. If they continue hiding at the sight of us, we take them to a monitored feral colony as soon as there's an opening.

We did not expect to get close to Xerox. Indeed, he wouldn't allow us to touch him. But from the first day, he watched us with bright-eyed interest. He didn't have the distrustful look of ferals. His vet visit was a challenge though. When we went to get him after he was altered, he darted off in terror and crawled inside a large piece of veterinary equipment that looked like a photocopier, hence his name. He recovered his composure quickly enough back at the shelter, and he was always in view when we were around.

After a short while we could reach a hand toward him and he'd bat at it, not aggressively but mischievously, before flitting away. Even though he wasn't a cat we could cuddle, Xerox became well known and beloved to the volunteers. He was an imp. By June, he had become such a friendly, flirtatious little guy that we knew it was time to list him for adoption. He reveled in being the center of attention, and he sat up straight and proud while you stroked him. We didn't try to pick him up. This mercurial little cat would have wriggled out of our grasp in a second and danced out of reach.

But he made friends with us and enjoyed our company. He talked to us in an excited little voice that sounded almost like a quack in his eagerness. He was captivating.

We had to be careful about adopting Xerox out. His exquisite beauty would generate interest from adopters. But he needed a home that could allow a skittish youngster time to learn trust while keeping him safely confined indoors. He also needed a home with other cats since feline company had been his social world since birth. In a home where he could bond with his own people, he should be allowing them to touch him within weeks and might even learn to enjoy sitting on their laps. He needed an adopter with a lot of patience and no expectations. Fortune smiled on Xerox when such an adopter came along at the end of July. We sent him home with a family that lived in a neighbouring community, and we waited to hear how he was settling in.

The news soon came. "Xerox didn't say a word all the way home," the adopter wrote, "and when we put the carrier down, our other cats did a pretty good job of ignoring it. One muttered something under her breath and left the room. The other sniffed the carrier a couple of times and then left the room too.

I didn't know what to do next, so I opened the carrier and left the kitchen. When I came back, the carrier was empty and there was no sign that Xerox had ever been there. We had closed off the basement, but the rest of the house was there for him to explore.

By Sunday evening, we hadn't seen or heard a peep out of him. We wondered if he crawled through a very tiny crack into the basement. We looked upstairs and down. Still no Xerox. After I moved all the boxes in our crowded attic and peeked under everything upstairs that could shelter a cat, John found him sitting in a hidden part of a bookshelf by the stairs.

We were worried that he hadn't moved all night and all day, so he had gone without water and food. I thought of how Katie's Place settled newcomers. We pulled out a large dog crate; put in a litter box, water bowl and food dish; found a box with "Xerox" on it in big, red letters; put the towel from Katie's Place in the box, and turned it so a cat could hide out of sight. John coaxed Xerox out from his hiding place and put him in the crate. All day, Xerox slept in his box, pressed against the back wall so no one could see a hair of him.

By Monday night, I wondered if he was ever going to talk to us. Then just after midnight as I read a book at the kitchen table, I heard a tiny sound and saw the top of a pair of ears appear and disappear. I looked back at my book and, yes, there was definitely a cat sitting on top of his box. If he sat up very tall, he could see me. He ducked down again, and I looked away. Next, there was a chirrup from his direction. Xerox was calling the other cats. No one came. (They had avoided the crate and the kitchen all day.)

What could I do? I opened the crate and sat back down to read my book. Our newcomer explored the kitchen and bathroom and then flew past me into the living room – and disappeared again for close to twenty-four hours. I began to wonder if this was going to work. Had he found some way to the basement? I took food and water downstairs, then came up and closed the basement door behind me.

That evening, all three cats were invisible. John went to bed leaving me at the table with a book. What was that? A noise upstairs? A tiny chirrup at the bottom of the stairs? Yes, there he was, calling to one of our cats to come and play. She looked at him and went back to bed. Xerox decided to come and talk to me instead. He hid under the table and gave some good Oriental yowls until I talked to him. For an hour, he went from room to room, finding out who was where. Some good, loud hisses from the bed. That would be Ting. A couple of minutes ago he paused at the library door to talk to me. Hooray! I think I'm accepted. Xerox is home for good."

So the introduction period passed successfully. That put our minds at rest. Semi-feral cats are hard to place in good homes, but this seemed to be working out. A couple of weeks later more news came and was even better.

"He has turned into a social butterfly, greeting all the T'ai Chi students just one week after coming home with us. He's decided that the laser pointer is his favourite toy, especially at night when he can race back and forth in the darkened living room catching that little red spot. Last night while we were watching a movie, he jumped on the couch and cuddled up between us. He tucked himself under John's arm with the biggest smile on his face, purring loudly, and spent the whole movie like that."

It was unbelievable progress after only a couple of weeks. We filed Xerox's adoption as complete and carried on tending to our animals at the shelter who awaited their own lucky chance.

More than two years later, we heard from the family again. Their note said, "Xerox thinks that everyone loves him, and he loves everyone back. He has developed into a wonderful Mao cat, apparently purebred, from his looks and behaviour. Though born feral, he has become the friendliest cat I've ever met. He has never met anyone – adult or child – that he doesn't like. He climbs into people's laps and wraps his paws around their necks, purrs like crazy and kisses them."

It's not often that skittish youngsters become so gregarious after they're adopted. They bond with their families, yes. But Xerox embraced every human he met. It was a triumphant outcome for a cat turned over to us as feral.

Edgar's Epiphany

Few shelters have space for cats with Feline
Leukemia (FeLV) and Feline Immunodeficiency Virus
(FIV). So when a rescue group called about a cat they'd
trapped and neutered who tested positive for FIV, we
took him. It was early September 2005. Edgar was black
and white, a sturdy, feral tom with the coarse appearance
of cat who'd lived rough. As soon as we let him out of
his new-cat cage, he took up residence in hidey holes on
the Boys' Pen porch, and we never saw him. We let him
be, aside from the occasional look to make sure he was
okay. Whenever we came too close, he growled, hissed
and spat as savagely as any wild cat.

One day, a volunteer tried to give him some treats.
She knew better than to put her hand into his lair, so she
tried tossing them into the opening. Edgar saw only the
arm swing toward him and he slashed at it with claws
bared, narrowly missing the hand. His snarl and a glint
of hatred in his eye made the volunteer think better of a
second attempt to win him over.

Inured to cold by long experience, he chose to spend winter on the porch, as far away as he could get from everyone. Five months passed without a sign of him coming inside. Then one day in March, a volunteer glanced into the Boys' Pen when passing by and thought she saw Edgar sitting on the couch. She turned back to look. It was indeed Edgar, and he was watching her with an inquiring expression. His face seemed much softer than the face that menaced us from the hidey holes on the porch. She entered the room, and he hurried outside. Other volunteers began seeing him indoors after that. Within a week or two, he felt bold enough to stay in the room when we were there too. We let him have his space and spent time with the other cats.

He began to gain confidence in us rapidly. We put treats under his nose without losing a finger; we gave him a stroke as he ate.... One morning, a volunteer went into the Boys' Pen for a short visit. The cats milled around her, clamouring for pets, and she stroked any furry head that found its way under her hand. Several times, she felt a broad head with a bent ear, so she looked down to identify its owner and saw it was Edgar. When she realized she'd been petting Edgar she stopped in surprise. He looked up with a face that seemed to ask, "This is okay, right? It's okay that I come for pets too?" She stroked him again, and he reached into her caress. The ice was broken. After that, he socialized with us more and more.

Edgar was never feral. He had been homeless for so long and chased off by so many people that he learned to fear humans. Property owners would have treated the big stray as a pest. Other cats became his family. He made friends among the Boys' Pen residents before he accepted us. He developed a particular bond with another reclusive, injured street cat named Bootsy Boy, and we often saw them grooming each other. Edgar was still a bit insecure in our company. But he had experienced a life-altering epiphany. In his time with us, memories of being loved by people resurfaced. After years of living in the shadows, he realized he was safe and loved again. He never returned to those hidey holes on the porch.

After February 2006, he would snooze on the couch or on the perch by the window, always surrounded by his friends, and always ready to greet any visitors. It was a new life for Edgar. We would never know what he endured before he was rescued, but we knew it had been hard. His ears were notched with battle scars, and one ear bent backwards at the tip, probably damaged in one of many fights for food or turf. The middle toe on his left forepaw flattened at the knuckle and pointed upward at the end, likely a break that healed badly. How on earth would a cat break one toe? It didn't matter. Edgar forgot the past in his ecstacy at belonging.

That spring, he was compulsive in his craving for affection. Like a river after a logjam breaks, his pent-up need drove him to follow us as he tried to make up for years of loneliness. If we went to pet Handsome, Edgar was there, insinuating his head into our caresses again. If we moved on to pet Gordie, Edgar was there, cheek to cheek with Gordie, trying to absorb some of Gordie's caresses. The others were tolerant of him, perhaps sensing that Edgar meant no harm and just had a profound need to fill.

Not before that winter did Edgar's neediness subside. By November, we were able to pet another cat without having Edgar at our elbow, hopping from one foot to the other in excitement while his weather-beaten face gazed up at us. He also included more cats in his circle of close friends. One evening, we saw Edgar and Gordie playing on the floor, wrestling like two big, carefree kittens. He became a member in good standing of the main social group in the Boys' Pen which included Milkdud, Peppermint, Randall, Sox and Bootsy Boy. Later, Felix and Porter would join that group.

We saw Felix grooming Edgar one day. He held Edgar steady with one paw and gave him a good wash. Edgar soaked it up and nudged the ever-patient Felix to continue if he slowed down. This group of tuxedo cats looked like a high society party, gray tabby Randall being the sole member not in black-and-white formal attire. The group often snoozed in one pile on the couch. When a visitor came in and sat down, they all crowded onto the lap together until they slipped off the sides. Sometimes Edgar ended up at the edge, clinging to the visitor's knees behind the other cats. The simple joy he took in what little he had endeared him to everyone.

A year passed, and the gang maintained their routine of snoozing together until they spied a free lap. But the FIV and Feline Leukemia took their toll in the Boys' Pen. We lost Milkdud, Peppermint and Porter. A long-haired tabby named Lucas joined the pen, and he found the confidence to climb into a lap before he felt comfortable among the other cats. For a while, Lucas was the first to reach a lap, and he spread out blissfully. If Edgar tried to inch his way on and got too close to Lucas's face, Lucas would give him a swat. That sent Edgar scurrying away. He wasn't a dominant cat and would give up a prize rather than fight. There was such a vulnerable soul inside that big, tough body.

In February 2008, Edgar had his first vet visit since arriving. He had always been robust, and the trauma we would have inflicted trying to crate him and get him to the vet for a checkup outweighed anything he'd gain. Evelyn worried that the trip to the vet's would upset him. He hadn't been out of the shelter in nearly two and a half years. But he was showing signs of trouble in the litter pan. He was about eight years old now and due for a checkup. Carefully, she enticed him into a carrier, and the visit was done.

She reported with delight his exemplary behaviour at the vet's. "Edgar was an absolute doll. He came out of the carrier, no problem, and purred like crazy during his exam. He was quiet and not worried while being palpated and poked. When I brought him back, he came out of his carrier with no hard feelings over the trip (unlike

Sox who ran away as if I was the devil). This makes me think maybe he would adjust to a home if he was adopted. I was very impressed with Edgar's behaviour today."

We hadn't listed Edgar for adoption because he'd taken months to trust us, and we feared a change in environment would destroy his trust again. But Edgar deserved a family to love him. So we listed him. The vet visit had revealed that he needed a dental. He seemed thinner, and he always wanted the soft food we prepared for another dental patient in his pen. It was possible that gingivitis was developing and made it painful to eat crunchies. When we listed him for adoption, we offered a permanent foster situation in which we would retain responsibility for vet bills.

Two months later, Edgar was clearly having trouble with his mouth. He drooled a lot and seemed quiet. His dental had just been done, having been delayed until we were sure a bladder infection had cleared up. Hopefully, the dental would help solve his mouth troubles. Over the next month, as May turned to June, Edgar remained quiet. He didn't rush to greet us these days. Since his bladder infection, he had come to associate the volunteers with syringes of medication being poked into his mouth. That would shake a cat's faith after he'd considered us friends. We hoped he would become his old eager self once we no longer medicated him daily. We had seen Boys' Pen cats through worse than this, and we looked forward to Edgar's usual fanfare of welcome when he rebounded.

One Saturday in June, the cleaning volunteers let themselves in first thing in the morning and began their work. The volunteer who took the Boys' Pen cats under her wing came equipped with her special formula of enriched cat milk. When she finished cleaning, she would pour a dish for each cat. They loved it and drank greedily. Knowing Edgar had been feeling low, she looked for him to see how he was doing. He wasn't in any of his usual spots. She searched all the hidey holes until she found him. He was curled up in a nest as though in a deep sleep. He had climbed in during the night, closed his eyes and passed away. Volunteers cried openly that morning.

Edgar's passing was unexpected. He had been doing well until the last few weeks. We learned from his vet visit in February that he was at the start of renal failure and a bit anaemic. But these conditions alone would not cause his demise within a few months. So we went ahead with his dental. Many other cats with FIV have bounced back and carried on for quite a while. Edgar, however, was getting on in years. He'd lived a hard life. Even though he was content among his friends at the shelter, he had grown tired.

He left as he'd arrived, alone. The difference was that he loved us, and he knew we loved him. The log book entry for June 21, 2008 read, "Edgar passed away overnight. Good bye, good friend."

He was beloved to us, this battered street cat who only wanted to belong.

The Cat Who Chose to be Wild

In June 2005, we accepted a cat that had been fed by someone for years. However, feeding was all the person could do. The postal worker on that route brought food so the man could feed Phoenix. Coping with other challenges, he had refused further offers of help with the cat. Over the years, the postie noticed her looking rougher and getting thinner. She grew matted and encrusted with purulant drool. He finally convinced the man that she needed and deserved more. Now she came to Katie's Place.

She was a long-haired gray cat in sorry condition – dirty and so matted that a couple of the mats were as big as her head. Her teeth were rotten, and our vet removed them all. No wonder her coat was in such bad shape. Grooming must have been an agony. It was a wonder she didn't starve to death. The vet estimated her age at about ten years. If she had ever been a house pet, it was long ago.

She hunched in a new-cat cage for a few weeks as she recovered from her dental, and we waited for any sign that she might regain trust in people. There was no sign. We had to let her out into the communal room. She promptly vanished into hiding in the rafters of the porch, the spot favoured by the shelter's ferals. Any sighting of her after that was of her retreating hindquarters as she hurried away at the sound of our arrival. For the majority of her life, other cats were the most family she'd known. She would stick with them, given a choice.

For more than a year, she lived at the shelter waiting for an opening in an appropriate feral colony. We kept an eye on her from a distance and were gratified to see her grow sleek and robust. Her thick coat grew in, and she lost the grim, beaten look we'd seen when she arrived.

In September 2006, she came down with an upper respiratory infection. We caught her and put her in a single-cat cage so she could be medicated through her food. Forced into close proximity with us for the first time since coming into care, she underwent a surprising change. Rather than shrinking back whenever we opened her cage door, she allowed us to touch her. Not only could we stroke her, she leaned into our touch. This response, after more than a year of hiding from us, was unexpected and unprecedented.

It seemed that dim memories of human love in a long-ago home had awakened. This cat was not feral. She had been neglected and maybe even abused at some time. She certainly suffered in her life. But she remembered human love and she welcomed it when we approached her slowly. The solemn expression on her face never changed, but we heard a soft purr as she reached for our touch.

She seemed content in the cage, so we kept her confined a bit longer after she recovered from the URI. We hoped she  might become so accustomed to us that she would stay in the human world after her cage was opened. Maybe she could find a home one day. She was an undemonstrative cat. It was hard to judge what she felt or when she'd be ready to release. We finally opened her door to see what she would do. She stayed where she lay. The next morning, her cage was empty and the somber little cat was nowhere to be seen. She resumed her place in the rafters of the Main Pen and never returned for our company. Even the kindness and caresses she enjoyed while confined did not tempt her to seek more.

In late December 2006, we rounded up some ferals at the shelter for transfer to a fenced, monitored feral colony on a volunteer's property. Phoenix was among the cats chosen. She had come as far as she wished to come in the human world. Her days were spent in the rafters of the Main Pen porch, and that was no way for a cat to live out her life. She deserved more freedom. Released into the cabin that was the ferals' main shelter, she ducked into hiding. When the volunteer returned the next day to feed and clean, Phoenix had left the cabin. All that would be seen of her now would be a glimpse through leaves from a distance. This was her choice. She was born among humans but was never loved enough to choose our company.

Two years passed, and the volunteer who looked after the colony was doing chores in the cabin one day. As she bent over some food bowls to refill them, she noticed Phoenix curled up nearby. She hadn't seen the old cat for a while and looked her over critically. That long coat had developed a few mats again. Slowly, she reached over to see if she could pull off a mat that hung by a few hairs. Phoenix lay calmly as the mat was pulled off. Curious about how far she could get, the volunteer put her hand out to give her a stroke. Phoenix allowed it and even showed signs of enjoying it. Before leaving the cabin that morning, she had given the cat a fuss just as she would to any pet in her house. Phoenix accepted the attention without showing any sign of craving more. For her, the contact had been a pleasant moment in a life that was complete without it.

She enjoyed the visits of the human who came to look after the place each day, even allowing her ears to be cleaned. The volunteer considered trying to integrate her into her home, but Phoenix appeared to be happy there. She had been seen exchanging gestures of affection with the other cats. At about fourteen years of age, it served no good purpose to uproot her.

On the morning of June 3, 2009, when their caregiver arrived to do chores in the ferals' cabin, she found Phoenix curled up in one of the nests. She had passed away in her sleep.

She was a gentle old cat who spent her kittenhood in a human home but never returned to human society, even when she knew she was safe among us. She had chosen the wild.

The Cat Who Disappeared

Ellie was a regal, long-haired gray cat whose family gave her up to a municipal shelter in a neighbouring community. She was angry at being left and did nothing to endear herself to the staff. She went from that shelter to a Petcetera store in hopes of finding a home from there. However, she probably sent that staff off in a disorganized retreat. From the Petcetera, she came to our municipal shelter where they decided she needed more time and space than they could offer. So she arrived at Katie's Place, grumbling and complaining, in late February 2004.

Finding herself surrounded by a new set of strange cats, Ellie seemed to decide that the best defense was a good offence, and she began a continuous growling grumble to warn other cats not to mess with her. Yet she yearned for reassurance. So between grumbles, she came to us and enjoyed some pets. The love session was punctuated by her occasional hiss to remind the cats that she was no pushover. But she returned immediately to nuzzling our hands.

She kept the other residents on their toes. Every now and then, volunteers heard mutters and growls as Ellie encountered something or someone who irritated her. The cats learned to give her space. After a few months, she settled down, and the grumbling was rarely heard anymore. She didn't come to us for affection, perhaps put off by the thought of running the gauntlet of cats to reach us. But if we went to her, she responded to a cheek scratch.

Six months later, Ellie was still a loner. She didn't hesitate to express her opinion, and her opinion was rarely good. She complained if another cat came close although we didn't hear the continuous symphony of growls we used to hear.

By 2005, we'd received no adoption inquiries about Ellie, and she seemed resigned to life among the feline rabble. She was a cranky diva who softened to sweetness in the rare moments that she enjoyed human company without interruption. Given half a chance, she would have been a lovable cat. To see that, people needed to overlook her attitude and her stern expression.

Spring 2005 came, and she had been at the shelter long enough now that in a bittersweet way she was contented. The daily bustle didn't faze her anymore. She claimed a tall, centrally-located perch as her own and minded her own business. Her perch kept her above the rabble and allowed her a good view of the whole up-stairs. Whenever we looked in, she was lounging on her platform, and the other cats knew better than to contest her right to it.

When autumn arrived, the balance in the room changed as the population changed. A spirited, one-year-old tortoiseshell now lived in that room, and she somehow won control of Ellie's perch. Now Gypsy Rose could be seen sprawled in the coveted spot, and Ellie was nowhere in sight. She had retreated to some dark corner for peace and privacy. It seemed that Ellie had met a cat she couldn't intimidate.

She lived more or less permanently on the porch that winter. Even when it snowed, that's where we found her, curled up in the big chair. She didn't look happy. People rarely visited her there in the cold weather, and no doubt she was lonely. Still, her only alternative was to join the crowd in the communal room. That, she would not do. We made a point of visiting her as often as we could. She brightened at the sight of us and stood to come closer for pets and strokes. Once we saw her playing out there, batting at some piece of debris she found under a bench.

The year turned and it was clear that Ellie had become depressed. She still spent her time hunched in the porch chair, and her face looked bitter. There had only been one adoption opportunity. We showed her to somebody, doing our best to promote her. Ellie did her best to

promote herself, rubbing and nuzzling. But the person said she didn't like gray cats. That was that. Ellie withdrew to the porch again. It was hard to see her rejected with no hope of getting out any time soon.

We decided to try her as a Barn Cat. She could live in the common areas away from the feline crowd. Currently, Mic was the only Barn Cat since Shamus voluntarily returned to the Main Pen for the winter. So we gradually introduced Ellie to the hallway outside her room. She was thrilled with her first afternoon outside and complained grievously when we returned her to the pen. Within a couple of weeks the transition was complete. Ellie now lived in the common areas. She still let us know when she'd had enough attention, but she became bright, interested and cheerful. The tension was gone from her posture and her face.

Those were good months for Ellie. She selected a shelf as her own and we placed her bed there. When spring arrived, we encountered a new problem though. The outdoors beckoned to her, and she discovered the dog door which belonged to the much-disrespected canine resident, Max. She used that door, and we could do nothing about it without locking poor Max in or out, or returning Ellie to the hated communal room. When we brought her inside, she put up an outraged protest and used Max's door to go AWOL again. But, after living so long where she never fit in, she was happy. Luckily, she seemed as outdoor-savvy as Katie who had roamed the territory around the barn since long before we arrived.

Ellie felt the call of the wild keenly. Some cats are homebodies and won't leave their own backyard. Others glory in the opportunity to roam and explore. Ellie was in the latter category. We'd see her throughout the day. In fact, she liked to greet volunteers in the parking lot when they arrived. But she began wandering farther down the driveway. At least she checked in with us regularly. We continued promoting her for adoption, and we had high hopes since she now presented a friendly face to visitors.

One morning she didn't show up for breakfast. We were more annoyed than concerned at first since it was a fine, warm September. We assumed she'd found better things to do than check in for breakfast. The volunteer who fed her scanned the yard but saw no sign of her. She had to finish her shelter chores and get to her paid job, so she left a note in the log book for the next volunteer to look out for Ellie.

The next person didn't see her either, and the notes in the log book became more urgent. A few days passed. We didn't even want to consider the possibilities. Pets had wandered that area safely for years, but a great deal of development began on 240th Street that year which might have driven predators closer to the shelter. We put up posters and waited anxiously. If someone turned her in at another shelter, we would be contacted when they read her tattoo. Our municipal shelter had no news of her.

We counted the days and scoured the surrounding territory. There was no sign of her and it was a tough thing to accept. We vowed to allow no further Barn Cats. Shamus was our only remaining Barn Cat, a status he'd enjoyed for years, and he stayed close to home. We had no other cats who were miserable in the communal rooms. They had enough hidey holes to get away from each other.

Ellie was unusual because she felt a wanderlust so deeply. The optimists among us wanted to believe she found herself a new home and the people just didn't think to report a found cat. Did we regret making Ellie a Barn Cat? On reflection, we'd have to say no. She grew so despondent in the communal room that she was unadoptable. The little sourpuss blossomed with her freedom. We had hoped adopters would notice the new cheerful Ellie. But it didn't happen. In another shelter, she wouldn't have lasted. She would have chafed at confinement among other cats wherever she went. Many shelters can only keep unadoptable pets for so long before they need the space.

Our new facility, built a few years later, was surrounded by tall, security fencing. Maybe that contained area would have been enough for Ellie. We still think of her.

The Cat Who Had Two Second Chances

Baby Bear wasn't a baby, but he thought he was. He came to Katie's Place with another cat named Meow in March 2006. Ginger tabby Meow was fourteen years old and Baby Bear was ten, a brown tabby with an angular face and large, Bambi eyes. He'd had the same home all his life and the two cats were loved very much. Allergies in the family meant the pets had to go. The parting was gut-wrenching for both the cats and their people. Meow was a calm, philosophical old girl who soon adjusted to shelter life. She had been adopted as an adult, so she wasn't surprised by the existence of a world outside of their house. She eventually went home with a volunteer and settled happily there.

Baby Bear was younger and had a better chance of being adopted. But he was also more traumatized by the loss of his home. He had been in the same place since he was six weeks old. He knew nothing about any world outside their house. The only other cat he'd known all his life was Meow, and he wasn't keen on meeting any new ones. He spent the first couple of weeks in their new-cat condo huddled underneath a blanket. The two cats weren't closely bonded anymore and Meow lay in her bed across  from a large, lumpy blanket. Peel back a corner of that lumpy blanket, and you'd see Baby Bear's doe eyes looking back at you.

With time, he recovered his confidence and realized he was safe in this new place. Once he was no longer an undercover cat, he sat on his perch and tried to catch our eyes, hoping we'd come and give him a fuss. He accepted the volunteers, but he didn't adjust to the other cats so well and he said uncomplimentary things to the cats in the next pen whenever he caught sight of them.

Within a few weeks, we moved him to a communal room where he expressed the same low opinion of his new roommates whenever they violated his personal space. He wasn't happy at the shelter, so we were delighted when a former adopter came by in June 2006 and decided to take the poor soul home. The man had adopted a cat with medical issues, and when that cat died, he was willing to give another special-needs cat a chance. Baby Bear needed the chance most. The adoption was completed, and it should have been a happy ending. But two days before Christmas 2006, the unthinkable happened. Baby Bear's adopter passed away unexpectedly.

The sensitive tabby came back to Katie's Place, having lost the second home he'd grown to love and where he'd been loved. He was frightened and miserable all over again, and he crept into a far corner of his old communal room where he huddled on a blanket and warned the other cats off. One of his roommates, Dior, shared Baby Bear's poor opinion of his own kind and they exchanged growls, each trying to out-growl the other. Again, we urgently wanted to find a home for him. This time a volunteer stepped up to adopt him. She had grown fond of the funny, tender little cat who always tried to put on such a display for the others. Home he went, hopefully for the last time in his life.

A year later, he was still enjoying what was truly his forever home at last. His person told us, "The General, formerly known as Baby Bear, is doing wonderfully well, and I can't believe we're only just coming up on our one-year anniversary together. He is sitting on my lap right now, resting his head on my arm and making it difficult to type, but do you really think I'm going to ask him to move? He is such an affectionate and adorable guy, and we're so glad to have him in our family." Baby Bear was once again the adored baby in a family, just as he liked it.

The Cat With the Sore Paw

Callaway's family turned her over to the municipal shelter in July 2006. She sat in her cage and regarded her new surroundings with a skeptical face. When people reached into the cage too quickly, she took it as an affront and made her feelings clear to them. Needless to say, she didn't have good prospects for adoption, so they sent her to Katie's Place.

She settled into a new-cat condo and seemed a little less disapproving of this latest change in her life. Looking us over, she decided to give us a chance. Within a short time, the fractious little cat was ready to make friends. She watched us hopefully when we arrived. Then if we came over to visit with her, she purred while reveling in all attention we could offer. Still, adopters showed little interest in this black-and-white cat with the bulldog chin.

She was affectionate and should have attracted interest sooner or later, but her chances were compromised in August when she developed a problem with her right forepaw. Now she was a plain, adult cat with a medical issue. How she injured herself was a mystery. She still lived alone in a condo. The vet had trouble pinning down the cause of her swollen ankle. He did a fine needle aspiration and it appeared to be cellulitis. But it didn't respond to treatment. It could have been an infection so he tried different antibiotics. If she didn't improve soon, she might need a biopsy on the fluid in her joint. Despite any discomfort, she still purred in a deep rumble whenever we gave her attention.

Callaway's problem had a comical side that she herself would not have appreciated. First, the vet had to shave her ankle to get a close look at it. She was a long-limbed cat with a thick, medium-haired coat. Now when she sat up, her broad chest narrowed down the length of her fluffy legs to a ridiculously-narrow, shaved ankle. Below the ankle, as skinny as a plucked chicken's, her fully-furred paw bloomed like a clown shoe as she sat with her toes pointing out.

That image was enough to make anyone smile. Then the vet wrapped her leg from elbow to toe in an enormous splint. It had to be big enough to immobilize her ankle joint. Callaway didn't understand any of this. She regarded the object attached to her leg with a bemused expression. All she knew was that a huge, stiff thing encased her leg, and it was annoying. So she shook her leg every now and then, and the splint rattled against the walls and floor with a resounding clatter, causing Callaway to look around in startled disapproval, wondering who was making the awful racket.

She handled her incapacity with aplomb. The splint didn't prevent her from doing anything she wanted to do. It was a minor irritation that she shrugged off. She still purred for visitors. When the vet decided it was time to remove her splint, she resumed life without a second thought. Her leg recovered fully and she walked with her old feline grace.

A few weeks later, we moved Callaway to a communal room where she settled among the other cats peacefully. She had an endearing personality. Her behaviour was a far cry from the affronted behaviour of the cat who dismissed strangers with a swipe when she was at the municipal shelter. She was a loving soul even if she wasn't the prettiest cat in the room.

After eight months in shelter care, one of the volunteers had grown attached to her and adopted her. The volunteer soon reported: "I just wanted to let you all know that Miss Callaway has settled in really, really well. I came back from a four-day trip on Sunday night to discover she had not only checked out every room in the house but decided my husband was her best friend. Funny, he in turn has become very attached."

That's how she worked. She could put strangers off with a haughty glance, but once you knew this sweet, funny character, you couldn't help but get attached.

The Cat Who Lost Patience Only Once

A plump, black-and-white cat arrived in August 2004 with the undistinguished name, "Fluffy." Her family simply didn't want her anymore. She was eight years old. Fluffy proved to be a good-natured, easygoing cat, and from the start she purred if you so much as looked at her. Blending smoothly into the population of her communal room, she spent her days watching the antics of the younger cats like a contented old aunt. We thought her age would make her hard to place, but five months after arriving, she found a home. The adopter was willing to take a pair of older cats, and Fluffy's amiable personality sealed the deal for her along with an equally amiable cat named Boomer.

The pair became office cats and lived at a pet food company where the staff doted on them. They enjoyed pampering from many employees, six days a week throughout that year and seemed to be set for life. But in one of those unforeseeable twists of fate, the company folded at the end of 2006. The people moved away, and the cats returned to the shelter.

They resumed residency at Katie's Place serenely. Boomer was a majestic, orange-and-white fellow who loved to greet visitors, and he was adopted quickly. Fluffy was close to eleven years old now, and her prospects were not as promising. She was friendly and healthy. But when hundreds of young cats need homes, a chubby eleven-year-old finds herself at the back of a very long line. This was only of concern to the volunteers. Fluffy herself was content wherever she ended up. She was a placid cat who whiled away the days in her nest, looking out at the world like a round, broody hen.

More likely than not, pudgy old Fluffy would be with us for a while. So, deemed unadoptable, she was designated a Barn Cat to live in the common areas of the shelter rather than in one of the pens. She chose to live in the new-cat cage that she had occupied at the top of the stairs, though we left the door open. She had her fleece-lined bed there and her food and water. It was her suite. She roosted in her bed by the stairs, leaving it only to waddle a short distance in aimless exploration when the spirit moved her.

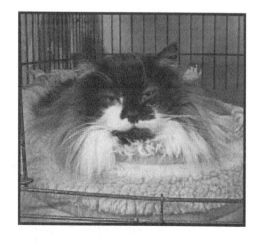

She wasn't very active, but she still had a typical feline nature. A volunteer was cleaning out a bunny cage one day and left a bag of hay open on the floor. In true feline fashion, Fluffy determined that this new object was significant to the humans and therefore required her to sit on it – or in it. It wasn't the most comfortable nest, but it was different and special. She looked a bit disconcerted when we reacted with laughter. However, her dignity was not offended enough to made her move. She stayed in the bag until we had to put it away.

Fluffy was a source of amusement again when she was shaved. Her long coat had become matted, especially in the areas a chubby girl can't reach to groom. The volunteers rarely had time to brush the long-haired cats enough and some were shaved periodically. Shaving confirmed there was more to Fluffy than fluff. She was as round without her long fur as with it.

Unflappable Fluffy tolerated almost anything without complaint. One event alone ever roused her to anger. She and a volunteer named Sandy were sitting together one day, Fluffy in her nest and Sandy on a chair by her cage. They had developed a bond over the weeks. While they sat companionably, a visitor came over and hoisted Fluffy out of her bed without preamble. She held her appraisingly for a moment and then plopped her back down like a sack of potatoes. Fluffy was affronted and her eyes were fierce as she smacked the visitor's hand in a rapid-fire series of whacks without claws. The visitor sniffed in disapproval and moved on. Sandy's eyes gleamed at Fluffy's spirit when she told the story to other volunteers after open hours ended.

Like the other volunteers, Sandy already had cats at home, and she feared tension in the household if she adopted another one. But her affection for the stout little cat had grown, and she began to worry that somebody else might notice what a treasure Fluffy was and adopt her. This prospect was unthinkable, so she took the plunge and completed the paperwork. Fluffy would have to adjust to a home with two other cats, one a feisty diva and one a former feral. But she had lived amicably among the cats at Katie's Place, as had the diva and the former feral before her. We were confident she would be fine.

Fluffy did indeed adjust, accepting her new circumstances as calmly as she accepted every other change in her life. The other cats' noses were out of joint at first, but they too adjusted. The old girl had been a family pet, an office mascot and a shelter cat. Now she had the forever home she deserved.

When the Light Went Out of Ashley's Eyes

Ashley was a dainty cat with a larger-than-life personality. A tiny, gray spitfire, she had a low threshold for stress. She was not unlike many humans in her eccentricities. Many of us prefer to avoid bustle and don't like sharing our living space with too many others. Ashley didn't have much choice when she was taken to the municipal shelter in June 2005. She had been found as a stray, but she didn't get along with her finder's kitten. So she ended up at a shelter which Ashley considered worse than sharing space with a pesky kitten. She made no secret of her opinions. Feeling angry and betrayed, she lashed out at everyone. In July, she came to us.

Katie's Place was another ordeal for Ashley who had to navigate a crowd of cats in her communal room. She would have preferred not to live with other cats, and she didn't hesitate to say so. She warned them away with shrill yelps when they invaded her personal space. Ashley needed a lot of personal space. What might simply annoy someone else set her off squawking in outrage. If another cat jostled her, Ashley viewed it as an egregious assault. She responded to people with a yelp and a swat, but only because she was stressed. She settled with time and became loving with the volunteers when she wasn't crowded by other cats. Between outbursts, she climbed into our arms and cuddled like a baby. She could be affectionate on her own terms. But she was a feisty diva and there's little demand among adopters for feisty divas. Over a few months, she adjusted and shared her communal room quietly with her roommates. We only heard the occasional yelp if she was run over by a reckless roommate.

Ashley couldn't show adopters her loving side during our busy open hours. When volunteers were alone at the shelter and it was quiet, she was a lamb. One said, "If you're near Ashley when she's on a chair, she reaches up with her paws on your chest until she's standing. If you stop lovin' her before she's had enough, she'll climb up on you again as soon as you turn your back."

She was an elegant little cat and people asked about her. Depending on her mood, Ashley welcomed their attention or merely tolerated it. The encounter always ended however with Ashley running out of patience. She never did any real damage, but the implication was that if we didn't leave her alone now, she might have to use force. That was enough to put people off. In truth, she was lonely. She longed for someone of her own.

One weekend in November 2006, Ashley was in a particularly good mood. That weekend, she greeted visitors with a beatific smile from her perch by the door.

She asked everyone for cuddles and enjoyed a lot of attention. On Sunday, a visiting couple warmed to her and found her charming. We told them about her, and they were unfazed by her history of unladylike behaviour. They decided that this appealing little spitfire was for them and completed the adoption. She would be their only cat. It was a heaven-sent opportunity. So Ashley was coaxed into a carrier, having refused, with shrill squawks, our offer to trim her claws first. We asked them to let us know how things went, and we looked forward to their report.

A week later, we heard from them. They loved her, and it seemed that she loved them too. She had just needed a home of her own in order to flourish. After a year and a half of shelter life, she was happy.

It should have been a happily-ever-after story. But a year later, her people had a baby, and Ashley found herself sharing her world with a noisy newcomer who stole a great deal of her people's time and attention. She couldn't adjust. Her life went into a tail spin with this sudden change. She became stressed and anxious, and she expressed her anxiety in an animal's way. She began peeing in the house. The vet offered her family Amitriptyline to calm her but they declined, and in May 2008, they returned her to Katie's Place instead.

Ashley was crushed. She thought the worst had happened when the little stranger took over her family. Then the catastrophic happened when they put her in a carrier and took her away. Her family said she was a fantastic cat when there were no other pets or new babies. We hoped we'd be able to find her a home on the strength of that testimonial. Evelyn took her for a new-cat vet check. The vet believed her behaviour was totally stress related. Bloodwork had been done recently and everything was fine. All she needed was a dental in the next couple of months. Evelyn told us she was so good at the vet's.

When Ashley lost her home and came back to the shelter, she was different. We remembered the spunky little diva who would give the other cats a piece of her mind. Quick to assert herself one minute, and quick to climb into someone's arms the next minute, she was always a spirited, confident cat. Now, although she still warned off other cats, the life seemed to have gone out of her. She seemed much older than her years and spent most of her time sitting quietly as though she had withdrawn into herself. If she'd been upset by the baby's arrival, she was bereft to lose her home. The spark was gone.

When she didn't seem to be her old self, we took her to the vet for another checkup and to get the dental that was recommended at her new-cat visit. They did the dental and discovered a lump on her gums. It was sent for biopsy. The results confirmed cancer, and they called Evelyn with the news. She wanted to take Ashley home to enjoy her last days with some one-on-one attention. But the vet was adamant that the cancer was advancing too rapidly. The recommendation was to let her go now. So Evelyn went to be with her. It was July 14, 2008.

Ashley lay curled up on a towel, and she purred and nuzzled Evelyn's fingers. Then as Evelyn held her and stroked her, she slipped away. It was the last tender

moment in a life with too few tender moments. In the
end, there was no place for this tiny diva to belong.
Technically, she lost her life to cancer. But if life had
been better for her, she might not have succumbed, not
so young. Weakened by stress and sadness, and without a
reason to fight, illness overcame her. Ashley was only
five years old.

An Unusual Adoption

All Gulliver and Janelle had in common was that
they were hard to place and were adopted together.
Gulliver first arrived in 2002 as a ten-month-old. Even
then he was a somber, introspective little cat who chose
to sit in a cubby hole and watch other youngsters play.
His youth and attractive, brown-tabby looks won over an
adopter. Confidence would come as he bonded with his
family. He did well, but circumstances changed in the
home, and he was returned to us in December 2005, now
an introverted adult who would be even harder to place.

He stayed out of sight in his communal room for
some time after arriving. Then, more and more, we saw
him sitting on the fringe of activities. He remained a
timid cat who enjoyed attention that was offered slowly.
If any kind of commotion broke out in the room, he'd
look worried and try to be invisible.

Janelle was one of several feral kittens trapped and
brought to the shelter in October 2005. They were on the
verge of becoming irreversibly feral. Some responded to
handling and went to new homes. Some never stopped

darting into hiding at the approach of a human and eventually went to our feral colony. Janelle was in the middle, neither accepting contact nor darting into hiding. She skipped away if we came too close and looked back at us with an expression that warned she'd run if we followed. She was exceptionally pretty with a torbie coat in vibrant colours. But since she steadfastly rejected human contact we had no expectation of finding a home for her and didn't list her for adoption. The hope was that she might mellow with age.

Months passed as Gulliver and Janelle each lived in different communal rooms, and the months became a year. Then in May 2007, a couple came to the shelter to find a hard-to-place cat. They chose Gulliver, to our delight. Then they noticed Janelle skitter across the floor when they entered her room. They told us they wanted her too. Taken aback, we explained her semi-feral status. They still wanted her. So we explained the special requirements of a semi-feral cat in a new home. They understood and were willing to do whatever it took for both cats to become confident family members.

Gulliver went into a carrier reluctantly. But crating him was easy compared to persuading Janelle into a carrier. When the paperwork was done, the family drove off with their hard-to-place cats and a lot of optimism. We waited for news of how this unusual adoption was working out. The family had our confidence, but a lot depended on the cats' personalities. News soon came in detailed reports. It was all good. Updates arrived over several months, and we read with pleasure of how this pair was integrating into their new home. The family told their story from the beginning.

"We left with very nervous kitties, Gulliver and Ellie (Janelle), and bundles of hope. Our hearts melted when we read about Gulliver who'd been at the shelter for one and a half years, a fact we still find amazing as he has such tremendous heart and tenderness! We adopted him with two-year-old Ellie, who wasn't expected to be adopted and had also been at Katie's Place for one and a half years.

We were both excited and curious about how they were going to adjust. The first night, they kept to themselves under the bed and were so quiet you'd never know they were there, as we expected. Gulliver was more than happy for us to reach under and pat him. Ellie kept her distance. The next day, we found that Ellie really likes to play (which lured her out), and Gulliver really likes attention (which lured him out).

Surprisingly, Ellie was the first to venture out of the bedroom, low to the ground. She had to pass Simon in the doorway, but she did it (very brave). Finally Gulliver did the same. We moved to the living room, and they soon appeared, peeking around the corner (at different times). Gulliver managed to make it over to us and stayed lounging around looking for attention. After several attempts, Ellie made it over and settled behind the couch. When we went to bed, they both appeared back in the bedroom. Ellie was still very quiet but, come the middle of the night, she seemed to be trying to break racing-around-the-apartment speed records. This morning, I peeked under the bed and they were sleeping beside each other. We are hopeful that they will bond."

This progress was a pleasure to read, and we were gratified by the family's tolerance of the cats' limitations. Later, another update arrived.

"It's been just shy of two weeks since we brought home the two little imps, and we are really enjoying them. Gulliver no longer darts away every time he hears a door close or a sound in the hall. He likes to sleep under the bed but does come out when we call him. Then he gives a big stretch and looks for a pat. He's like the gentle big brother to the crazy little sister. Ellie is a fun-loving monkey. She likes to be where we are, but if we reach out to her, she zips away. She has arched her back into my hand, then zipped away as if surprised by herself. We also think she loves to dash by us as a game of thrill and daring. Ellie uses her happy meow-chirrup when she sees Gulliver and when she trots by us too. So we think we're in her clan.

We are hopeful that Gulliver will become more comfortable with the affection Ellie displays for him. He seems a bit nervous when she gives her attention to him, so he sometimes gives her a little bat. Her latest trick is to race around dragging a three-foot-long soft toy behind her. Gulliver seems to love chasing after her. Of course, we wonder if it's another luring-Gulliver trick she's found."

A month later, the next update arrived, and we were surprised by how fast Janelle was bonding with the people.

"Gulliver spends his time in proximity to us (instead of under the bed), and he no longer bolts for the safety of the bedroom when he hears sounds outside. He greets us within a couple of minutes after we arrive back home. We've also seen him play a bit, and we wonder if playing is something he's never really done, so he's learning this art. (He watches Ellie play a lot.) Ellie is like a shadow at times, following us around. We can pat her now, and sometimes she flops on the ground for more pats. Nothing seems to scare her. The vacuum cleaner is just something to investigate. They're wrestling buddies, and Gulliver lets Ellie curl up beside him more and more. It's like 'little sister' pestering 'big brother.' Sometimes it works, sometimes not."

Clearly this adoption was a resounding success. Seven months passed, and the last update arrived.

"We can't believe these two little rascals have been with us for a year and a half. Hiding under the bed is pretty much a thing of the past. It only occurs with Gulliver when the vacuum comes out. Ellie, on the other hand, thinks the vacuum is something fun to chase and stalk. We still haven't mastered the art of picking them up, but that's okay. We keep telling them, 'we're going to practice getting picked up,' but they zip away. Instead of being scared, I think they might be laughing at the slow humans. We can do it, but we don't get far. We plop them back on the ground, and they both flop over, looking for a pat.

Gulliver has become a relaxed little dude with an entertaining range of meows, especially if he wants a pat when we wake up or walk through the door. He's

channeling
his inner
kitten more
and more. He
used to act
surprised at
himself when
he tentatively
chased a ball,
and if one

rolled up to him, he'd skitter away. But now, we throw a ball and he goes after it like a shot. He seems to love racing around, just in a more dignified style than Ellie's rough-and-tumble style.

Ellie ambushes us for pats, as does Gulliver. They have a habit of planting themselves in our paths and not moving until they get pats. It's like they have a secret Pat Toll thing going on. Both have mighty big purrs, and Ellie has a special meow when she's looking for Gulliver after the vacuum scares him away. They're a far cry from the timid little ones we brought home a year and a half ago."

The Cat Who Was a Prankster

A wiry, tuxedo cat was turned in at the municipal
shelter in July 2003, but they couldn't get close enough
to touch the frightened animal. They named her Crystal,
and when she didn't relax after several days, they
deemed her feral and turned her over to Katie's Place.
We took the cat straight to the vet for a new-admission
checkup. He advised us that Crystal was not an appropriate name, so we changed his name to Kris Kringle. Kris
was set up in a new-cat cage at the shelter, and we
waited to see if his hostile attitude would thaw. Every
time we peeked into the carrier he used as a bed, he was
pressed against the back of it with his ears flattened,
glowering at us and hissing.

After a while, it was clear that this cat wasn't getting any friendlier in confinement so we let him loose in
the Main Pen. He promptly vanished into the shadows of
the room. We only saw him from a distance after that.
We were accustomed to dealing with ferals and didn't
expect more contact with him unless we had to round
him up for a vet visit.

We did see him in different nests around the room though. One thing no cat could resist was a toy at the end of a stick that we waved for them. The stick created enough distance for the ferals to feel comfortable, and all the cats were mesmerized by the toy dancing on the string. Right at the front of the group following the toy was Kris. He became so focused on the bouncing object that he forgot to treat us with disdain and he cavorted like an eager kitten. Playfulness was Kris's most defining characteristic. More precisely, he was a prankster.

He wouldn't let us touch him, but ultimately this was by choice, not due to fear. Before long, he would come right up to us when he could catch us unawares. He would leap to a shelf just over our heads and grab at our hair with his paw. Still we had no idea how mischievous this cat could be.

The new-cat cages in the Main Pen were latched with long metal pins. We laid the pin on the shelf above the cages whenever we opened one. Several times, volunteers apparently forgot where they left it and were unable to latch the cage until they'd scoured the area for the pin. They were always puzzled to find it far from where they'd been working. This happened to more than one person on more than one occasion. It seemed as though we were suffering from some kind of group dementia.

One day a volunteer was sweeping by the couch while another scooped litter in the new-cat cages. She put the broom down and turned in time to see Kris sneaking past the other cats, belly low, making his way toward the cages. The other volunteer was bent over a litter pan, unaware of him. When he reached the shelf where the pin lay, he pulled it the last inch toward him with his  paw, picked it up in his mouth, and silently made his way to a high shelf where he dropped it at his feet. He gave it a half-hearted bat or two, but his objective had been to steal it, not to play with it. He sat with it at his feet and looked smug as he waited for the volunteer to begin searching for it. That was the part he enjoyed. For a while, we were all careful with the pins since Kris waited for us to leave them unattended. But he tired of the game when he knew we were on to him.

Kris had come into his own. He was a confident, cocky little busybody who poked his nose into every-thing. He always seemed to have a scratch on his face from butting into another cat's business. He was bright and he was restless. One Saturday, he amused himself by leaping across the doorway from one shelf to another just as people were entering. It startled them when a small form flashed past their faces. Kris would turn to watch their reaction with merriment in his eyes. If they went closer to see the mischievous cat, he waved his paw as though challenging them to a duel. For him it was one big game.

He still had a defiant streak that made him hard to adopt out. One volunteer spent quite a bit of time with him, and they developed a bond. He accepted her as his particular friend. But poor health took her away from volunteering, and Kris returned to the outskirts of the feline group that hung around us.

He was a capricious soul. One day, a visitor met all the cats and remarked to a volunteer about the cute, playful, black-and-white one. He pointed to Kris Kringle. Kris was in his I'm-a-friendly-cat-come-and-see-me mood. On another day, a volunteer tried to approach him but he flitted out of reach, casting irritated looks over his shoulder. He was in his I'm-a-feral-cat-leave-me-alone mood.

By August 2007, Kris had been with us for four years. He seemed content with life at the shelter. He was able to find enough mischief to get into to keep himself amused. His roommates viewed him as a nosy pest, annoying but nonthreatening. The volunteers were all well acquainted with this flamboyant cat, but he kept his distance from them and was no trouble.

In early August, a lady dropped by who had adopted hard-to-place cats from us before and who fostered semi-feral cats for shelters to socialize them. She had room in her home at this point for two more cats, and we talked with her about which ones would be best to go home with her. In the end, she chose Kris Kringle and a depressed, aloof little tortie named Mia. Mia only needed a real home and a consistent human presence in her life.

Kris considered the shelter home, but he was an energetic young cat, too young to live out his life in a shelter.
The lady knew Kris from way back since she visited
often. Something about the independent little cat touched
her and he stayed in her mind. So today, we agreed, was
the day. She deftly loaded him into her carrier, outwitting
him in his game of Evade the Human. He protested his
capture with plaintive meows which tore at her heart.
She couldn't wait to get him home and settled. Soon he
was set up in her bedroom with the necessities. Then she
came back to complete the paperwork.

Kris might be a handful, but this was a cat-savvy
home and probably the best chance he would ever have
for a good life outside the shelter. He would have much
more space to poke around, and there would be other
cats to tease. That was all this cheeky character wanted.

The Cat Who Just Wanted a Lap

Misty was taken from her home when her person became ill and began mistreating her without realizing it. She had been loved, and it must have been as difficult to see the change in her person as it was to lose her home. She was taken to the municipal shelter in late December 2005, frightened and confused. As an older cat who was sensitive by nature, she didn't recover from the upheaval quickly. She would have been lovely with her dilute tortoiseshell colouring, but her face was a mask of dour mistrust. There was little hope of adoption for her, so they transferred her to us.

She didn't settle at Katie's Place much more happily than she had at the municipal shelter. For the first couple of weeks, she huddled in the back of her cubby hole, warning everyone with hisses to keep their distance. We were encouraged when she finally came out and lay on a shelf in the communal room. She was uncomfortable around the other cats though, so she was reluctant to move around. If another cat confronted her, she cowered in terror. But they left her alone on her shelf at the end of the room, and there she stayed. She never ventured out of her area, never acknowledged people's arrival and never asked for attention.

She sat with solemn dignity, looking about as cuddly as Queen Victoria. She didn't betray any uneasiness in her posture. The one sign of unhappiness was her somber face. Because she seemed relaxed but disinterested in company, few people paid attention to her. She was the invisible cat, curled up in a corner. So we were surprised to see her respond eagerly when someone did give her affection. She stood and reached into a caress, nuzzling and showing more liveliness than anyone had seen in her yet. Before our eyes, she changed from a reserved and inconspicuous cat to a loving, perky cat who glowed under our attention. When we left, she settled back down and withdrew into herself again.

She rarely had company so she didn't expect it and didn't ask for it. With many other cats clamouring to be noticed, it was too easy to forget about her. But once she recognized someone as a person who had been kind to her before, she would stand and look hopeful when they came in. If she even suspected that you might be heading her way to give her a fuss, her face would brighten.

If only somebody was interested in adopting a quiet, older cat. Some adopters wanted a cat who would be good with their children. We couldn't promise that Misty would be. Others wanted a cat who would be frisky and playful. We couldn't promise that either. This cat was lonely and needed a home, but her prospects were bleak.

In February 2007, when Misty had been with us for more than a year, we were contacted by an extended care facility. One of their residents wanted to adopt a quiet lap cat to live with her in her room. We thought of Misty. This chance seemed to drop from heaven for her. We set a date to bring Misty to meet the lady who was in a wheelchair and couldn't come to the shelter. Now we just had to hope she would like the cat we'd chosen. We knew the lonely cat would respond to anyone who showed her affection. But few people gave the solemn old girl enough time to warm up.

Soon the day arrived to take her to the facility, and two volunteers set out with a disconcerted Misty inside a carrier under protest. Ushered into the bedroom, they opened the carrier on the floor and coaxed Misty out, praying that she wouldn't become frightened, start hissing and hide. She stepped forward and paused at the carrier door. She seemed to be considering turning around and going back in, but the volunteer kneeling by the carrier quickly began stroking her. Arching her back into the touch, she stayed out for more. She looked dubious though and scanned the room. Many months had passed without her ever leaving her corner, so this was quite an experience.

The lady was eager to meet the cat we'd brought. Without further delay, we picked her up and placed her in the lady's lap. She smiled and put her hands around Misty as she stood in the lap watching the doorway. The two volunteers held their breath. After a brief, undecided moment, Misty settled down across her knees and showed no inclination to leave. The lady stroked the little cat, beaming with pleasure. Misty licked her hand. They sat like that for many minutes, enjoying each other's company. After a while, she tried to put Misty on the bed beside her. But Misty turned and crept right back into her lap. The elderly lady never said much but her smile spoke volumes. This was a match made in heaven. All she wanted was a lap cat, and all Misty wanted was a person to love her. The volunteers left them together and returned to the shelter with the carrier swinging, triumphantly empty, in one volunteer's hand.

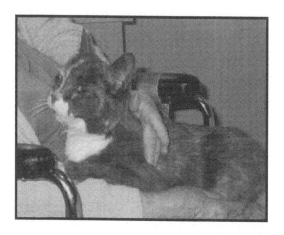

A Cat Who Had a Guardian Angel

Satchmo was taken off the streets in September 2005 by a kind person who took him to the vet and ensured that everything he needed was done. Then they took him to the municipal shelter. But he cowered in mute terror within the protective walls of his litter pan, unable to even lift his head. He was too terrified to be adoptable so they turned him over to Katie's Place.

We set him up in a new-cat cage where he lay in a tense ball at the back of the carrier he used as a nest. His eyes stared ahead, bleak and unseeing. The poor cat was likely feral and would have to be released into a colony. But we give every cat time in the shelter first, just to be sure. The vet estimated his age as one or two years. He was in such sad condition that any time spent in human care could not have been long.

Soon after he arrived, we found we could stroke him. So he wasn't feral. He accepted the touch meekly. Only his eyes moved, showing the conflict he felt at allowing contact. It was possible that he was just a timid, sensitive cat. He may have suffered abuse or neglect in his past life that made him fear people. We wanted to see if we could win his confidence.

At the end of September, we saw signs of progress. He still huddled in his carrier-bed without moving. But one day he tried to communicate. A volunteer had reached in to stroke him. He flinched but didn't turn away. She rested her hand on the bedding in front of him and touched his paw with a finger. The paw touched back before pulling away. Then he took her finger in his mouth and held it for a moment, an odd little gesture. He was still nervous. But he had responded.

Within a week, he reached another milestone. The first volunteer to arrive at the shelter is always greeted with a chorus of meows. You learn to recognize them and you know who's talking to you. But one persistent meow was new. Following it to its source, the volunteer found Satchmo standing at the door of his cage, calling for some attention. He had been spending more and more time sitting on his carrier-bed rather than inside it. He was still not completely at ease. He enjoyed a head scratch and meowed, then hissed, an almost unconscious action that betrayed his lingering anxiety.

Another week later, Satchmo seemed to realize he could trust us. He became a lively, friendly cat who watched everything from his perch on top of his carrier-bed. When we called to him, he answered; when we went to his cage, he stood in anticipation of some pets. He lovingly mouthed the hand that caressed him, his own gesture of friendship. Sometime in Satchmo's past, there might have been a person he loved whose hand he held in his mouth as part of their ritual of affection.

In October, he was ready to leave his new-cat cage and join the communal room. There was still a chance he would disappear into hiding and forget that human contact was pleasant. But a cat could only be kept confined for so long. At the appearance of a visitor the next day, he was just a black flash scuttling for cover under a chair. While the visitor spent time with other cats, Satchmo seemed to remember that he was among friends. He crept out and jumped to a shelf. Lying across the shelf, he stretched out a paw toward the visitor. A few caresses had him rolling and reveling in attention again.

Satchmo grew not just comfortable with people but eager for human company. He liked a chair by the wire because it allowed him to lean over the back of the chair and watch for us. A few times, he climbed over the back and descended between the wire and the chair with his legs splayed like a large, furry spider. He'd become a clownish little character. If we went into the pen, he rolled and wriggled with such enthusiasm that he'd fall off the chair. Then he hurried away in embarrassment. One volunteer said, "He bats my ponytail when I'm kneeling to give Valentino his insulin shot."

Months passed and Satchmo's hunger for attention subsided to normal. By May 2006, he was no longer as anxious to see us arrive. For a while, he'd always watched and waited by the pen door. Now he was usually occupied elsewhere when we came in. But if we went to him and gave him a few pets, he soaked it up as blissfully as ever, rolling onto his back and waving his paws in the air.

Adopters never inquired about the plain, black cat, and Satchmo didn't bother courting their interest. By January 2007, we had moved him to the larger room downstairs, the Main Pen. He was content but didn't bond with any other cat, and he wasn't afraid to take a stand in a confrontation. One night, we heard a brief ruckus which ended before we could see what caused it. The upshot was Mojo streaking across the room to a shelf on the far side while Satchmo sat with an incriminating tuft of Mojo's fur sticking out of his mouth. He was a sturdy fellow, and the other cats would have been well advised to avoid annoying him. But with people, he melted into a wriggling bundle of happiness.

He made the best of life as a shelter cat and spent most of his time meditating. Adopters could not be persuaded to consider him. Although he was young, he had a craggy face that could not be described as cute, and the stocky build of an intimidating tom. Then in August 2007, nearly two years after he'd arrived, he found a home. Someone came to the shelter one Saturday who wanted to give a chance to a couple of cats who needed it. This was one of those special people, a person who was not looking for love but who wanted to give love.

Satchmo and a black ten-year-old named Angus were the cats she chose.

Satchmo's story had come full circle. As a kitten, he'd been somebody's pet. Then some event left him homeless, and terror made him so unapproachable that the staff in his first shelter left a question mark by "Male/Female." For many plain, black, adult cats in many shelters, that would be the end of the story. They can't compete with all the attractive, sociable cats. Satchmo caught a lucky break in a hardscrabble life when he was rescued and ended up at Katie's Place.

His new person dropped by a few weeks later and told us he was doing very well and was "such an affectionate cat." Indeed, he was a plain cat with a guardian angel.

An Incorrigible Cat

Cubby, a twelve-year-old, gray-and-white cat, lost his home in August 2003. He didn't adjust well to shelter life so we wanted to find him a home quickly. However, he had two strikes against him. He was a senior, and he was hypersensitive. Cubby was anxious to be noticed among the other cats and anxious to make friends with people. He did not, however, want any cats near him. Cats made him anxious too.

Living in the Main Pen, he slashed at every cat who came within three feet of him and he made life miserable for them. So we put him back into a single condo and began beating the bushes for a foster home. He wanted people to visit him. When someone did go to see him, he was so overwhelmed that he didn't know what to do with himself. He nuzzled their hand and smacked it in the same moment. He paced, gulped a crunchie, nuzzled, grumbled, and then smacked again – the very picture of restlessness.

He needed a home with no other cats and just one or two adult humans. But there are too many good-natured,

youthful cats looking for homes. The odds of Cubby
finding one were remote. So he lived alone in his condo
and we visited with him, ignoring his grumpy-old-man
routine, while the search for a home continued.

Autumn passed and his attitude grew worse. He
began lashing out at volunteers when they opened his
condo door. Clearly he was neither happy where he was,
nor adoptable. Any foster homes already had cats (and if
Cubby hated other felines, nobody wanted him among
their own). His personality was deteriorating from the
frustration of living in a small space. He reacted with
violent agitation more and more when we opened his
door. One day in December, he bit a volunteer in a frenzied moment.

We had run out of options. We'd never euthanized a
cat for aggression and we didn't want to start. Animals
are logical for the most part and don't attack if they feel
safe and their needs are met. Cubby needed space. The
Boys' Pen was the only area with space. It was a last
resort. If he harassed the residents in that pen, we would
have few options left for protecting the other cats, the
volunteers, and Cubby.

We introduced him to the Boys' Pen one morning
and watched to see how he'd take it. He stood for a
moment, looked around, and then crept for cover. While
we watched, a couple of cats wandered close to sniff the
new scent. Cubby grumbled but only lashed out when
one leaned in closer. Once we were certain the introduc-
tory period had passed without incident, we carried on
with our work. Cubby remained wary but quiet that day,
the worst confrontation being some grumbles that

reached fever pitch when he ventured out of his hiding place and passed another cat.

The integration was successful. No stalking; no attacks. He left the other cats alone unless they came too close, and they learned to give him space. We were soon able to stroke him. He waited for us and looked forward to his evening treats, rubbing against the wire in antici- pation.

The next spring, several new cats joined the Boys' Pen. Cubby adjusted to the influx well. He considered the shelves around the door his personal territory. As long as the other cats respected this, he ignored them. He whacked a few unwary volunteers but never bit anyone again.

He loved seeing people arrive. As soon as someone came through the main door, he hurried to rub the wire and strut back and forth on his shelf. He was thrilled with attention but could handle very little stimulation before needing a break. A smack was inevitable. Yet he seemed surprised if we recoiled from him. He had no compre- hension of his own hostile behaviour.

The volunteers learned to work around him. If your work took you into his personal space, Cubby assumed you'd singled him out for persecution and he would flap and complain. One day, a volunteer needed a broom from behind Cubby. She moved her left hand, and as he tracked the motion, she reached behind him with her right hand and walked off with the broom leaving Cubby bewildered.

Overall, he was content with his life. A particular hobby of his was watching the chickens and rabbits from a porch shelf. He adored treats slipped to him by volunteers who deftly pulled their hands away while he gobbled the tidbits. He would grumble at any passing cat, head butt the nearest surface in appreciation of a visitor, and then glare in grumpy-old-man fashion. That was contentment, Cubby-style.

On Christmas Day 2004, he suffered some kind of episode. He was uncoordinated and easy to handle for longer than the few seconds he usually allowed us. Because it was Christmas and he was in no distress, we decided to just monitor him. He seemed to improve over Christmas although he lay quietly and purred as we stroked him. This mellow, affectionate Cubby was unsettling. The vet diagnosed a soft tissue injury and thought he might have fallen. He recovered and was soon back to swatting and grumbling. His high shelf was accessible to him again.

That shelf belonged to him (according to Cubby). It was close to the ceiling lights and was warm, a luxury in midwinter. One cold evening, a brown tabby named Gordie decided he wanted that shelf above the door. Cubby wasn't around, so Gordie made himself comfortable. Then who should come wandering back but Cubby. Seeing his shelf occupied, he sat down behind Gordie and glowered. Gordie's back must have been burning. Judging from the look of grim determination on his face, he knew Cubby was there but refused to be chased away. After several uncomfortable minutes, Gordie decided he'd made his point and left with studied casualness. Cubby settled in his customary spot and forgot about Gordie. He was no longer the aggressor he'd been when he arrived.

Summer turned to autumn in 2005, and he started showing his age with moments of apparently senile behaviour. We saw him discipline his own tail one day, vexed by its movement while he was grooming. He was hunched over, licking his belly. Just beyond his face, the tail waved as though it had a mind of its own. Cubby evidently believed that it did, and he took a swipe at it, uttering a warning growl. He resumed grooming, but the insolent tail continued waving in front of his face. Again he swiped at it. In the end, he gave up the grooming session in exasperation.

The year passed and 2006 arrived. Cubby sat by the door as always and called to people. We would intercept visitors and warn them of cats they should leave alone. But occasionally we missed somebody. Cubby would nuzzle the wire, meowing prettily as though saying, "Oh please come and see me, I love having visitors...." People might push a finger through the wire to scratch his head. They were always surprised when, two seconds later, the sweet entreaty became a rebuke with Cubby swatting the wire and grumbling as if to say, "Oh why are you subjecting me to this persistent and relentless attention, you rude and insensitive person!"

Confrontations between cats sometimes happened when we entered the pen. They always gathered, hoping for a fuss and jostling each other in their rush to the visitor. Cubby sometimes joined them, either hoping for a treat or still believing he liked attention. One day, a big fellow named Handsome hurried up behind him and didn't notice Cubby until too late. Cubby had turned to face him, grumbling with outrage and waving a paw hysterically. Handsome weighed twice what Cubby weighed and had a coat so thick that no claw could penetrate. But he was such a mild-mannered soul that he shrank back and retreated. That probably made the silly curmudgeon feel invincible, at least for a moment. With the attention span of a fruit fly, he forgot the incident immediately and found something else to complain about.

Despite his blustering, confrontations never came to blows. We had taken in another cat that we thought should have Feline Immunodeficiency Virus (FIV). This young male grew up with a cat who tested positive after they had shared a home for some years. Yet he tested negative. It brought to mind a phrase experts used in describing the transmission of FIV and Feline Leukemia. "Prolonged and extensive cat-to-cat contact" was needed. Cubby avoided any contact with other cats. The literature said that sharing bowls and litter pans over time could pass on the viruses. That had not happened with the young male. We couldn't help wondering if Cubby might still test negative.

In March 2007, we had him tested during a routine vet visit. He was negative for both viruses. How would that affect his future? His chance of adoption was negligible. He was about fifteen years old, and the Boys' Pen had been his home for more than three years. We decided that nothing should change for him now.

Spring 2007 saw him as lively and cheerful as ever, at least by his standards. He still muttered peevishly when something annoyed him, and something always annoyed him. A big, docile, ginger cat named Rufus arrived and claimed the perch below Cubby's. It annoyed him that Rufus claimed territory so close to his own. But he ignored Rufus unless his head moved within reach. Any moving object in Cubby's range would get a swat. But Rufus didn't even seem to notice.

Occasionally, the younger cats took liberties such as Peppermint did one day when she decided to take a shortcut. The cheeky youngster leapt over Cubby as he lay on a shelf, and he didn't so much as blink. Perhaps this was a sign of advancing age.

In September 2007, our old curmudgeon wasn't looking well, and his crotchetiness was replaced by sweetness. A vet visit revealed that he had a tumour and didn't have much time left. We arranged with the vet to come to the shelter and help him pass. Scheduling euthanasia is one of the hardest things we do. We don't want an animal to suffer needlessly, but we also don't want to end a life too soon.

The vet came, and after looking at Cubby's alert face and seeing him tuck into his food, she said we could wait a little longer. The decline would be gradual, and the best indicator would be appetite. Over the weekend, we gave him extra food and treats. He was never in discomfort, just quiet.

On September 26, he lost interest in eating and started to crash. Evelyn stroked him as the vet eased him from life. He had been with us for four years and one month. We hoped his last years were good. He would have preferred a real home. But he had many friends, and he was loved for his irascible character as much as in spite of it.

One Cat Who Was Lucky and One Who Was Not

Simon and Sabby lost their home in May 2007 when a young family member began developing an allergy to them. Sabby was born in June 1996. Simon was born in November 1995, and that had been the only home they'd ever known. Finding themselves at the shelter terrified them. They didn't want to leave the safety of their carriers, so we left their doors open in a new-cat condo, and they crouched there for the rest of that day, looking out with wide, stricken eyes. Simon was a large, leggy, black-and-white fellow, and Sabby was an exceedingly-plump orange tabby.

For older cats, they adjusted quickly. Within a few days, they were coming up to greet people and ask for some pets. Simon was a bit bolder than Sabby. She managed to find the courage to come forward and join him in getting a fuss. If she heard a noise, she scooted back to her nest. But once they both settled in, Sabby proved to

be the most
affectionate of
these two very-
affectionate cats.

    They lived
in a large condo
at the top of the
stairs, and Sabby
watched the
volunteers' every
move in case one
might decide to
come and visit with her. Hearing someone climb the
stairs set her off purring in anticipation. By the time we
reached the top steps, her purr reverberated around the
room. When we looked over at their condo, there was
Sabby's round face watching hopefully. Simon didn't
wait at the door, but when we gave him pets he rolled
over and wriggled like a silly kitten.

    They would be hard to place since they were seniors
and a bonded pair that had to be adopted together. Com-
plicating that were health issues. Simon was fine, but
Sabby needed daily medication for mild heart disease
(although our vet ascertained later that her heart was
fine). Sabby had also been known to have the rare acci-
dent outside the litter pan, which pretty much sealed
their fate as far as adoptability went. At twenty-four
pounds, she was chubby. So her problems were probably
weight related. However, the issues that made them hard
to place were offset by their wonderful dispositions.

That summer, we had a lead on a home for them and only needed to wait until the person returned from vacation. But we never heard back although we left a message asking if they were still interested. We had been holding off moving the pair to a communal room. It would have been best for them to go straight to a new home without adjusting to a new room first. But now we moved them from their condo to a pen where they could enjoy access to a porch. They settled well and greeted us as eagerly as ever. Sabby welcomed us at the door with a low-key happy dance, strutting with grace and delicacy for such a large girl. They hungered for affection, particularly Sabby.

In November, another lead on a home came along. But Sabby's health had deteriorated. She had lost weight over the past few weeks and seemed lethargic. An x-ray revealed something above her heart that didn't look normal. The vet was unable to determine exactly what it was. She needed to be stabilized with her appetite restored. Then the mass could be x-rayed again for changes. So Evelyn fostered Sabby and supervised her diet.

She seemed contented at Evelyn's, erupting into purrs as soon as she was spoken to or touched. But she refused to eat. Evelyn tried every kind of food. It was critical that she eat, or she would succumb to Fatty Liver Syndrome. Evelyn force-fed her squirts of mushy food from an eye dropper, which Sabby didn't appreciate at all. By December, we were optimistic since she seemed to begin eating a bit on her own. Still, whatever happened, Simon would have a home if this latest lead panned out, even if he had to go without Sabby.

Sabby only nibbled sporadically, but she seemed comfortable. She played, grabbing her catnip mouse and chewing its tail. Yet she looked thin and tired. With New Year's Day came a turn for the worse. She became lethargic, she had difficulty moving and her breathing was laboured. It was clear that any hope of recovery was gone. Our vet went to her foster home on January 2, 2008, and she slipped away in her own nest. The vet explained that a tumour on Sabby's lung had eventually restricted the amount of oxygen getting to her body.

She seemed so robust when she first arrived at the shelter. Her purr used to fill the room. She had so much love to give, but she needed somebody to want that love. In the shelter, she couldn't get as much one-on-one attention as she needed. Her health wasn't the best and she lost any resilience when she lost her home of eleven years. Whether an animal loses a beloved companion or a beloved home, even the best shelter cannot make up for that.

Simon remained at Katie's Place. His hopes of getting that new home we'd counted on were fading because we hadn't heard from the person who inquired. We left a phone message, but they never returned our call. It was the second lead to go nowhere. Simon seemed happy though. Unlike Sabby, he seemed to thrive at the shelter. Lively and chipper, he waited for us at the pen door when we arrived each day. He didn't know what he wanted more, a fuss or some treats. Either way, when he saw you coming, he was ready. If he saw that bag of treats in your hand, he could barely wait for you to get through the door.

Six weeks later, a stroke of fate, both sad and lucky, landed Simon a new home. It was the day after Valentine's Day 2008. A fostering volunteer, Margaret, had taken home the surviving partner of a pair of senior cats several years ago. One of the pair, fifteen-year-old Sheba, had died of a large abdominal tumour three months after coming to the shelter. That left fourteen-year-old Meggie alone.

It was a scenario very like Simon and Sabby's. Meggie found a home with Margaret and was pampered until the day she died in February 2008, a month after Sabby. Sad as it was to lose old Meggie, her passing became Simon's good luck. He went to share Margaret's home with her other cat, and we knew he'd be as pampered as Meggie was. If he ever missed Sabby, with the simple wisdom of animals, he didn't dwell on it.

A handful of cases like Sabby's have convinced us that the shock of losing a home and family can trigger a weakness in an animal's constitution to become a full-blown illness. If they could remain in their homes, they might succumb to disease eventually, but maybe not for several more years. We rejoiced for Simon, and we wished we could have done more for sweet, gentle Sabby.

When a Broken Leg Was a Lucky Break

In late February 2007, we were called by someone who had been feeding a stray cat for quite a while. It was a long-haired silver tabby with tawny highlights. He must have been a fine sight in his prime, but homelessness had taken its toll. One day he arrived for his meal dragging his hind leg. Then he didn't show up for two days. His survival would have become more precarious with his injury, so when he reappeared the woman contacted Katie's Place.

She had never been able to touch the cat and assumed he was feral. However, she managed to lock him in her kitchen. A volunteer went to help capture him, and the panicked cat darted around the kitchen despite his injured leg, lunging at the window in a desperate bid to escape. Finally she maneuvered him into a carrier and took him to our vet.

The vet discovered that Lucas, as we named him, had broken his leg a couple of weeks ago. He either caught it in something or was hit by a car. It had begun to heal and nothing more needed to be done. But he also tested positive for Feline Immunodeficiency Virus (FIV), another risk for cats struggling to survive on their own. So he came to live in the Boys' Pen. He limped, and his left rear foot never rested flat on the ground again; his toes remained elevated when he sat. Otherwise, he suffered no lasting effects from the injury.

At first, Lucas stayed at the back of his carrier-nest and regarded us suspiciously. Within a week we were able to touch him. After a while, we opened his cage so he could melt into the population of the pen and avoid human contact if he wished. Yet he lingered in the cage, enjoying the security of a private suite. His eyes had lost their guarded look, and a curious volunteer tried petting him. To her surprise, he reached into the caress and beamed at her. Then he meowed conversationally. Apparently he was enjoying the chance to make friends. So much for being feral. Within another week, he was greeting us with a chirrup.

Lucas fit in at Katie's Place with all the delight of a cat who went from having nothing to having everything. If he had come from a home, he would have been miserable. Pets who lose their home struggle with the loss. Lucas behaved as if he'd won the lottery. He had dry, soft beds. Bowls full of crunchies were always available. People brought him plates of canned food, and they stroked him and told him what a fine boy he was. Yes indeed, Lucas thought he'd hit the jackpot. He didn't join the throng of cats who milled at our feet when we arrived. But if we called to him, he'd come over and soak up all the attention we offered. He never went out to the porch though. Six years of being outside was plenty for Lucas.

The vet estimated his age as about eight years. He had been seen around the residential complex cadging handouts for about six years. So he lost his home when he was a couple of years old. For only a small part of his life had he felt safe and loved. He was likely left behind when his family moved, a common scenario. Landlords find cats in vacant apartments. People see a neighbour's cat after the family has gone. If it doesn't leave the property, new occupants drive it away. The new residents will be the first of many property owners to shoo the stray off. Over time, a pet can lose trust in humans as Lucas had.

But now that he felt safe at the shelter, he was thrilled to be there. It was a toss up whether he enjoyed the affection or the food more. A volunteer arrived one day and found him by the food mat. She began petting him and he basked in her attention with evident pleasure. Yet he stole a few longing glances over his shoulder during their visit. As soon as she turned to leave, he hurried over to the bowl and ate. She realized he had been about to have a snack when she'd arrived, creating a dilemma for him.

Lucas chose a tall perch in the middle of the room as his own. He rarely left that perch for a long time after arriving. One reason was probably that it was a secure island from which he had a good view of the other cats without being among them. For years, he'd been on his own. Before that, he might have been the only cat in his home. So, although he had no argument with any other cat, his high perch created a comfortable distance. The second reason was that people always seemed to end up standing close enough that he could reach out and get their attention. If you stood  anywhere near Lucas's perch, you'd feel a paw on your shoulder or a furry head butting your face.

Eventually the perch was too grubby to keep and we replaced it with a new one. The replacement didn't measure up. Either it didn't have the right cachet for Lucas or he was ready to come down and mingle. From then on, we saw him sprawled on the couch with the others more often. He also began to enjoy lap time.

By the end of that year, Lucas still craved affection. After many years alone, he hungered for love with a fierce urgency. As soon as anyone came into the room and sat down, Lucas appeared beside them and settled into their lap with a look of deep contentment. The other cats wanted lap time almost as badly, and one or two might find a spot in the lap without being under Lucas's nose. But if they did get in his face, he swiped at them. We had seen him snuggle beside other cats for a nap, but he preferred people to cats, given a choice.

Lucas was such a lovable character that if any cat from the Boys' Pen were to be adopted, he was an obvious choice. Visitors were enchanted by him, and the volunteers adored him. On January 20, 2008, it happened. He went home with a family that volunteered at the shelter. They were hoping he'd fit in with a gentle little FIV+ cat named Rojo that they took as a Permanent Foster in January 2005. The family also had a dog that Lucas needed to accept. If he proved to be possessive, he would put his placement in jeopardy.

Sometimes, in his hunger for affection, he drove other cats away from a lap and settled there himself as though he intended to stay forever. Indeed, if the owner of the lap decided to leave, Lucas could get grumpy. We worried that he might try to dominate human attention in his new home and find his furry backside right back in the Boys' Pen. Only time would tell.

Two weeks passed, and the news from his home was good. His young person wrote, "Lucas is settling in very well. There was a bit of conflict between Rojo and him at first, but they're slowly warming up to each other. The dog isn't too fond of him but I think she's just afraid of him. At first he chose places to hide, but now he sits on the couch, or sometimes Rojo even lets him share the blanket in front of the fireplace. All in all, he's a really friendly cat, and even my dad, who didn't want another cat, has grown attached to him though he won't admit it."

That was Lucas for you. He had a way of winning someone's heart even if they started out indifferent. After six years of homelessness and nearly a year in the shelter, it seemed Lucas had a home and a family again.

The Boomerang Cat

Over two years, Mindy was adopted three times and returned three times. Yet she was young, healthy, attractive and one of the most affectionate cats we'd ever met. Mindy's flaw was her temperament and the fact that she detested other animals. If she got close to another creature, she turned into a bristling bundle of outrage. Being in shelters, surrounded by other animals, she had too many opportunities to display her dramatic streak. She would have been fine in a home with no other pets. Her particular adoptions were just bad luck.

She first came to the municipal shelter in July 2006 as a skinny tortoiseshell stray with kittens. She was a loving little thing who leaned into a cheek scratch, enjoying all the attention people could offer. But if she spied another cat beyond her open cage door, she would give him an earful of unladylike language. Staff and volunteers assumed it was the hormones of motherhood still making her hypersensitive. Mindy waited for a home for quite a while. When visitors came in, she stood in her box, purring and waiting for them to come and see her.

But everyone passed her by. Summers are a hard time for an adult cat to be homeless. Kittens are abundant and they're stiff competition for the few available homes.

Eventually the perky little cat was adopted. Several months later, her new family brought her back to the shelter claiming they no longer wanted her because she was too fat. They must have overfed her themselves. She had still been thin from nursing kittens when she was adopted. Perhaps the real reason was a hygiene issue that results from being overweight. Chubby cats have trouble reaching their hindquarters to groom. But that's not what they said. "Too fat" was the reason given.

It was a grim turn of events for a cat who never showed well among other animals. The other occupants of the shelter set her off hissing and howling at the sight of them. With little to do but eat while waiting for a home, she never lost any weight either. If anything, she became more rotund. Months went by, and someone else gave her a chance. Soon her second family decided they didn't want her either, and they returned her to the shelter. Apparently her behaviour toward other animals changed their minds even though they were warned of this before adopting her. It was now July 2007.

She was still affectionate with people. When someone entered the room, Mindy would stand and knead the cage floor while she purred in happy anticipation. She nuzzled her cage bars, willing visitors with all her heart to come and see her. She pressed her cheeks into people's hands, enjoying all the pets she could get. Everyone was enchanted by the plump, lovable tortie. But when she noticed another cat as she leaned out to nuzzle, she reacted with shrill howls and raised hackles. So much for the image of sweet innocence.

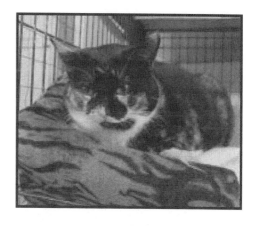

After many weeks of volunteers promoting her to adopters, she was given chance number three and went home with a family that believed they could help her adjust to other pets. They returned her the next day. Her reaction to other animals was more extreme than they expected. Again, the people were warned, but they underestimated Mindy's flare for drama. She had run out of time now, so she was sent to Katie's Place as unadoptable. This still wouldn't get her away from other cats, quite the contrary.

We installed her in a new-cat cage outside of the communal rooms, and that became her home. Her cage was at the top of the stairs, and after a settling-in period, we left the door open so she could stretch her legs. She saw other cats in the pens around her, but to our relief she showed no reaction to them. Given enough time in an unchanging environment, it seemed that Mindy could adjust to some proximity to other cats.

She accepted her circumstances. A cage as her own private suite was satisfactory, and she settled contentedly into a routine. She spent most of her time curled up on her bed. But if anyone sat in the chair beside her cage, she stepped into their lap right away, placed her fore-paws on their shoulders, and nuzzled their face with heartfelt kisses. It was an endearing gesture that won her staunch friends among the volunteers, and it won her a home. We made a video of her doing this and posted it on her web page.

A lot of inquiries came in. One, for example, asked, "Do you think that Mindy would definitely NOT work out with a dog and a cat?" Our reply did not mince words. Then in April 2008, the cat who had been adopted and returned three times was adopted for the fourth and hopefully last time. Someone fell in love with her on the web and came all the way from Richmond to meet her.

She did not disappoint her visitor. As soon as the young lady sat down in the chair beside her cage, Mindy climbed into the lap, put one paw on each shoulder and licked her neck. Then she curled up for some lap time. There they sat for quite a while, enjoying each other's company. The adoption was completed. Her adopter wanted a lap cat more than anything else, and there were no other pets in the home. This fourth adoption took. Mindy didn't return. Nearly a year later, we received a note from her new family letting us know that she had adjusted to her new home quickly and was doing great.

A Category Five Hurricane

Hurricane Katrina was named for her temperament. When she came into our care, she was a frightening force of nature indeed. In June 2007, staff at a recycling depot phoned one of our volunteers, Kathy, and told her a young cat had been abandoned there. She was pregnant and allowed the staff to put her in a carrier, purring the whole time. There was no inkling of things to come until after they gave her some food. Worried that they shouldn't have fed her yet, they took the dish away. That was when Katrina assaulted her first human.

Kathy arrived, and they gave her the news that less than an hour after they'd phoned, Katrina gave birth to five kittens in the carrier. Kathy left with the tiny tabby mom and her babies still in the carrier. Katrina allowed Kathy to pet her through the slats so, confident that she was well socialized, Kathy settled the little family in her bathroom and went to her shift at the shelter. She phoned her husband to let him know about the cats but couldn't reach him. He was destined to become the second human assaulted by Katrina.

Kathy's husband returned home while she was gone and wanted to use the bathroom. While he was there, Katrina shot out of the carrier on the floor and bit him on the leg. Not learning from this, he leaned over to pet her. That was when she tore into his arm. Now he retreated, harbouring black thoughts about his wife.

When Kathy returned she went to check on the little mom. As soon as she entered the bathroom, Katrina came barreling across the room, tail puffed and screaming obscenities. Kathy almost didn't get out in time. She then put on the thickest overalls she could find among her husband's work clothes, a heavy jacket and gloves. Armed with a large litter scooper to protect her face, and a broom to keep Katrina at bay, she returned to clean up the mess. Katrina had flipped the water and food bowls during her assaults.

The frenzied cat attacked the broom and launched a couple more assaults on Kathy before she could back her into the carrier and clean up. Later she realized that, having only one bathroom, she needed to move the mom and kittens to a spare bedroom. So she suited up and went back in. Again, Katrina launched an assault. One of the babies had been lying on her tail, and when she flew out of the carrier, he was tossed to the bathroom floor. Kathy managed to slip him back into the carrier while fending off Katrina with the litter scooper. There is definitely some kind of serious postpartum thing going on here, she thought, and hoped she'd never again deal with another cat in this frame of mind.

In the morning, Kathy checked on her furry guests, wearing full battle gear of course. While Katrina was engaged in reducing the broom to splinters, she took a quick look in the carrier. The kittens were okay as far as she could see. That afternoon, she took them to the vet's and noticed that one of the babies had died. She left Katrina and the remaining kittens with the vet for another foster volunteer to pick up, thinking, brave woman, as she headed home to restore order in her house. Kathy would be out of town for the weekend, and her husband had expressed great reluctance to be left with Katrina.

This was the story Kathy told us, and we felt some trepidation about what awaited us when Hurricane Katrina was ready for the shelter. Evelyn had taken over from Kathy. Since Katrina was in no mental condition to be a good mother, and her babies seemed to be neglected, Evelyn began bottle feeding them. However, more kittens died. They may not have been able to survive even if Katrina nurtured them herself. They might have had a congenital abnormality. They might have been victims of the same stress that caused their mom to deliver in the carrier. Katrina was a tiny cat and maybe she didn't have it in her to deliver a healthy litter. Despite the best efforts of this volunteer, experienced with newborn kittens, they all died within days.

After a couple of weeks, Katrina mellowed from a Category Five hurricane to a Category Three. She was still quick-tempered, but she no longer attacked in a blind frenzy. Perhaps the trauma of being rounded up and crated induced labour and also sent her over the edge. We'd never know. But it had been unavoidable.

Stressed by everything that happened to her and the maelstrom of maternal hormones in her body, Katrina probably didn't know if she was defending herself from captors or defending her kittens from strangers. She just followed her urges. Now, slowly, she seemed to be recovering and was calm enough to bring to the shelter.

We put her in the Main Pen. She was the smallest cat in the room by far. Yet she kept the others on their toes because she was still a hypersensitive little thing. She yelped hysterically if any cat came too close at first. She wanted affection and reached into a caress. But she quickly became overstimulated. Within seconds, she drew back and swatted. She never did any harm with her swats. She just wanted the handling to stop. We posted her story on the web in search of a quiet, cat-savvy home without children or other pets.

Despite her high-strung nature, Katrina was attractive. She was dainty with luminous eyes and a pert face. A visiting couple expressed interest in her one day. We told them all about her and, weighing her history against their own observations, they decided to adopt her. We hoped she would become a calm, happy cat in her own home. It wasn't to be. Three months later, she was returned. Her behaviour was exemplary until her family acquired another cat. That set Katrina off all over again. The fact that they gave her up rather than the new cat told us a bond hadn't formed. It just wasn't the right home. We didn't know if there ever would be a right place for this little diva.

By mid-December 2007 when she had been back for a couple of weeks, she was eager for affection despite her characteristic high tension level. She seemed to have mellowed since her first stay at the shelter. She would push your hand away a couple of times but she still came forward for pets. We moved her from her new-cat cage to the Main Pen at the end of December. She settled surprisingly well. We expected to hear squawks of outrage as she encountered various cats. But all was calm in the Main Pen. She still lost patience quickly with being handled. Yet she rolled flirtatiously, seeking more attention, and even showed a playful streak, prancing across the floor after a toy one day. She just had trouble with overstimulation when the shelter was busy. We expected her to be one of those cats who would be with us for a while.

Early in April 2008, a young woman came looking for a kitten. We didn't have any, but she met the cats anyway and was drawn to Katrina. The little spitfire had settled down and only got upset if another cat invaded her space. Otherwise, she was playful and friendly. The woman expressed serious interest in adopting her, and again we found ourselves explaining her history to an adopter. She listened thoughtfully, stroking Katrina's head at intervals. Katrina was well behaved except for a couple of moments when she fidgeted and pulled away.

After the story was told and the woman had given it some thought, she gave us her decision. Katrina was the cat she wanted. There were no other cats in the home, and we had described the consequences of a new cat coming into Katrina's last home. We felt confident this adoption would work. That day, the cat who had once assaulted everyone with murderous intent went meekly to a new home, her last new home.

The Perpetual Kitten

Gordie was a youngster when he came to us, and a
youngster he remained – irrepressible and happy-go-
lucky. A rescuer discovered him living on the streets
when she was tracking a different cat in September 2005.
While searching the alleys, she came upon a rangy little
tabby scrounging in a garbage can. It was clear from the
look of him that he'd been scrounging to survive for a
while. He was in decent condition generally, but he
tested positive for Feline Immunodeficiency Virus (FIV),
so he came to Katie's Place.

Released at our shelter, Gordie had trouble making
sense of it all. He had found himself scooped up in the
middle of a scrounged lunch and taken to a vet. Then he
went from the vet's to Katie's Place, which seemed to
him to be full of large and not-so-welcoming cats. That
first day, he got too close to Handsome who gave him a
swat. He hurried away in his confusion, looking like he
wanted to cry. His pitiful expression tugged at a volunteer's heart, and she gathered him up to console him.
Like a child clutching its mother's knees, he pressed

himself against her, finding comfort in her arms. When she put him back down, he rolled over to show his scrawny belly for as long as his anxiety let him. He wanted to show his new friend a gesture of trust, but he had to keep his eyes open for other cats. A mixture of bravado and vulnerability, Gordie could have melted the toughest heart.

Within a few weeks, he established himself as a member in good standing of the Boys' Pen gang. In fact, as cats arrived and left, he ended up being top cat in the pen, not by virtue of his dominance but because the others at that time allowed him to be first. He was first to greet a visitor, first to come for treats and first into a lap. As soon as anyone sat down, Gordie bounded into their lap out of nowhere. Then other cats joined him, conducting themselves with restraint compared to his unfettered exuberance.

If you wiggled your hand or waved a toy, he went instantly into play mode. He was a full-grown one-year-old who knew nothing of gentleness. You could end up scratched but, unaware of his gaffe, he'd look at you questioningly if you snatched your hand away. Gordie was just an uninhibited goof having fun. He had only one greater love than fun and cuddles. Untroubled about good manners, he'd drop you like a hot potato if somebody appeared with a package of treats.

He was also blithely unaware of his impact on other cats. A dainty, black female named Hope lived in the Boys' Pen at that time. One morning she was snoozing in a basket by the window. Gordie decided to join her. She was tiny, and the basket was tiny. So it was like watching an elephant wade into a kiddie pool. Gordie stepped in beside his little pal and began trying to make himself comfortable while she dodged his shuffling elbows and paws. Finally, with a sigh of contentment, he was settled. Hope was nearly squashed beneath him. All that could be seen of her was her head by Gordie's left shoulder. He seemed to believe she was as happy as he was, but it was too much for Hope. She burrowed out from underneath him and sat down on the other side, barely fitting into a basket full of Gordie. He grabbed her in an affectionate bear hug and began licking her. She looked uncomfortable but resigned. There was no denying Gordie.

He was happy with his life. Maybe it was just his unquenchable good humour that made it look like a good life. He en-joyed his food and warm nests. He enjoyed his friends and visitors, and he enjoyed the sunshine on the porch. One day we saw Gordie

and Edgar play-wrestling like two big kittens. They both came from wretched circumstances, and all they knew of comfort was what the shelter offered. It was more than they'd had before and they were glad of it.

Just once did we see Gordie behave with sober resolve instead of indulging his whims. Grumpy old Cubby had claimed the warmest shelf next to the light fixtures as his own, and all the cats respected this. But one January day when Cubby was elsewhere, Gordie decided to enjoy a little of that warmth himself. While he was relaxing, Cubby returned and, sitting down behind Gordie, he fixed him with a baleful stare. Gordie's grim expression told us he was aware of Cubby but refused to be intimidated. He stuck it out for several minutes before deciding that his point was made. Then he stood and left with slow, haughty dignity such as we never saw from him otherwise. Once he reached the floor, he was his giddy, goofy self again as he flipped onto his back under a perch and sharpened his claws upside down.

By May 2007, this Peter Pan cat seemed to have matured a bit. He was quieter for longer periods. He still had his moments, such as when a new cat arrived in their pen one day and we left the open carrier on the floor. Once the new resident was out in the room, we picked up the carrier to take it away. But it was occupied. Gordie had been unable to resist snooping.

His childlike innocence still surfaced at times. While others, feline and human, seem to know what behaviours are frowned on, Gordie blundered along, going where the spirit moved him. He joined some other cats on a visitor's lap one day. Throwing himself across the lap in front of Sox, he used Sox as a pillow and sprawled face to face with the visitor where he commanded her attention. He was a good-hearted cat, not competitive or conniving. It just never occurred to him that he might have cut someone off.

Adoptions from the Boys' Pen increased in 2008 as more people became aware of these cats' exceptional personalities. So it was no particular surprise when, in March 2008, someone inquired about Gordie after reading about him on the web. They came to meet him during our Saturday open hours. Gordie was as friendly and chipper as ever and made a good impression. On Sunday, they came back to take him home.

It's hard to guess how much animals know. They read signals we're not aware of sending. So Gordie might have realized he was home at last. They told us how he walked out of the carrier and began exploring his new home, "purring like a lion" the entire time. Despite his cheerful nature, we never heard Gordie purr at the shelter. A week later, they sent an update that said, "Gordie's favorite things are being the center of attention, sleeping under blankets and covers, and jumping up on window sills to look outside. He is just a big baby that loves to get petted and cuddled, and he is a beautiful, regal-looking cat too." The one thing that surprised us was the image of Gordie as regal looking. But even perpetual kittens can muster moments of dignity.

The Cat Who Wanted to Come Back to the Shelter

Lucy never had a home, but in a way she was never without one. She was trapped with her mother and brother when the youngsters were about eleven weeks old. These little black cats with topaz-coloured eyes lived in a crawl space under a house, and the landlord threatened to board up their entrance with the cats still inside. The tenant contacted us, and we rescued them. It was November 2002. The mom, a former pet, was relieved and grateful to be among people again. An affectionate cat, she was soon adopted. But her kittens had never met humans and had no wish to meet any now. They were well on their way to growing up feral. The siblings lived in a condo at the shelter and skittered away when we went in. However, in a small enclosure they couldn't skitter far, and they learned to tolerate touch, merely cringing instead of skittering.

After a few weeks they grew bolder. If we were in the pen next to theirs, a small, black paw came through the wire as Lucy tried to get our attention. One day, someone came by who was captivated by Lucy and Linus. The woman assured us that her last two cats were feral; she understood them and wouldn't mind being unable to hold them. She adopted the pair, agreeing to keep them in her bedroom until they settled. But she decided later that this was unkind and gave them the run of the house. A few days after adopting them, she called to say they'd gone up her chimney and what should she do? We managed to recapture the pair and bring them back to the shelter, grubby and traumatized. So much for that adoption.

It was a major setback. Linus, who started out as the more outgoing sibling, never allowed humans near him again. The two of them grew up at the shelter viewing humans as alien. They made friends among the other cats and, while Lucy eventually allowed us to stroke her, Linus kept his distance, watching us with cautious eyes.

By 2004, when they'd reached adulthood, Lucy was quite affectionate, running to us for pets and talking nonstop, although she still didn't like to be held. Linus remained aloof and disappeared into the rafters of the porch when we arrived. He found his niche among the feral cats who avoided us as completely as they valued each other's company. He and Lucy were following different destinies.

In November that year, the owners of a stable contacted us about taking some feral cats. We visited the property and were impressed. We had some ferals who would adjust well to this life, and the owners agreed to confine them until they bonded with the property, and to provide food for them. Choosing which cats to take wasn't difficult. Linus was a clear candidate. He was still young and should not spend his life within shelter walls. At the stable, they would have access to the acreage around the buildings. Their longevity could not be guaranteed, but we believed that freedom with its attendant risks was what nature intended and what the ferals preferred. Linus would have his friends around him and would never again have to hide in the rafters, waiting for us to leave.

Lucy, on the other hand, made friends among a family of cats at the shelter who were semi-feral and considered humans entertaining if not the kind of creature you want touching you. These cats were always nearby while volunteers worked. Lucy idolized them like a little sister, nuzzling and following them around. They allowed it but didn't initiate the contact themselves. Lucy was clearly lower in the hierarchy. One of the semi-ferals, Wannabe, grew more trusting over time. He was Lucy's main hero. So her trust also grew. In fact, she surpassed her friend in learning to trust. If we

crouched down, she hurried over and circled us, brushing us and gazing up with a look of adoration that she'd previously reserved for her feline friends. She grew more and more confident with human contact until she began jumping into laps for a cuddle. We knew it wouldn't be long before someone asked about adopting her. But Lucy's was an exceptional case. She would need a cat-savvy home and feline companions.

In early March 2005, one of the volunteers was ready to take some animals into his new home, and he settled on Lucy, Wannabe and a house cat named Shadow. Of the three, Shadow was the only one with a human home in her past. It would be a big adjustment for Lucy and Wannabe who grew up at the shelter. But, like Linus, they were young and deserved more than to live out their lives in the shelter. They all enjoyed human company so we had high hopes. However, the adjustment was harder than anticipated.

The volunteer who adopted them didn't have as much experience as some of us and he was anxious about them. Wannabe purred on good days, but Lucy became a hissing recluse in her new home. We tried reminding him of Hank and Houdini's adoption. These semi-ferals took several months to integrate at their new house, yet they became loving lap cats. Our reassurances weren't enough. He had agonized about adopting the right cats, and he agonized over their unhappiness with him. Six weeks after taking them home, he brought Lucy and Wannabe back.

While their adopter was tortured by his decision, Lucy and Wannabe resumed life at the shelter with nonchalance. There was no period of painful readjustment. As early as the next day, a volunteer reported, "Lucy was back to her same old self, winding around my legs, purring like crazy and looking for scritches." Another volunteer said, "Wannabe and I had a snuggle session last night, and Lucy was pitter-pattering around." They picked up where they left off with old friends and never looked back.

Although Lucy had long been full-grown, there was still something childlike about her. She could melt our hearts when she gazed up with that sweet face, and she still idolized Wannabe. One day, we watched as Wannabe meandered around the porch trying to decide what he wanted to do. Lucy followed him, hopping from perch to perch to keep up. He decided he'd go and have a snack. So Lucy joined him at the bowl of crunchies. Wannabe seemed a bit annoyed at being shadowed. When she leaned in for a crunchie, he cuffed her lightly. But the moment passed, and they carried on together with Lucy trotting behind him as he wandered off.

In March 2008, a couple came to meet some of the cats listed on our web pages. They didn't know about Lucy. After her abortive adoption, we didn't relist her. When the lady sat down in the Main Pen, Lucy hopped onto her lap and enjoyed all the attention she could get. Three times she hopped into the lap, and the lady was enchanted. She asked about the little cat and we explained, expecting her to carry on looking at other cats. Lucy's story was interesting, but there were more adoptable animals to meet. Yet the lady lingered in the Main

Pen, reluctant to leave Lucy who snuggled in her lap. Finally she said Lucy was her choice.

We hurried to a quiet corner and debated. One side said Lucy deserved the chance and shouldn't grow old here. The other side said there were cats who wanted to get out while Lucy might just end up coming back. In the end, Lucy was given the chance. It remained to be seen which side was right. She had spent her five years of life at Katie's Place except for two brief, failed adoptions. Volunteers on both sides were anxious.

We waited nervously until we received a note ten days later that described Lucy's introduction to her new home. "We made her a little cave under a chair in the bedroom, and she sleeps there during the day while our other cat, Noah, is napping. Did you know that she snores like a sleep-deprived trucker? It's adorable! Anyway, early evening, she trots out and goes to harass Noah. The two of them have become real little hooligans! She is still wary of us and hides when we're around, so we let them have the run of the house. All we hear is them talking to each other and thumping as they play and run after each other. She seems to be getting used to us though. She doesn't slink with her belly quite so low. I am quite smitten with my Luce Goose and am so relieved that she has adapted so well. We can't understand why the person who adopted her previously said she hissed so much."

This hardly sounded like our Lucy, the lovable but timid little cat who considered Katie's Place her real home. We still half expected some setback that would cause Lucy to be returned.

At the end of April we received another message from the family. "The last week has seen the best and biggest change. She has just about reverted to the Lucy I met at the shelter. Last night, for the first time, she jumped up on the bed and smothered me with affection."

Obviously Lucy wasn't pining for her old life. She only needed the right home, and she had found it.

A Boisterous Bounder

Skittles was an impetuous cat, and he was big. He lost his home at the age of seven, ending up at a municipal shelter in September 2006. He wasn't happy when his life turned upside down, and he let people know it. He was friendly enough, but he reached his limit quickly and had tantrums like an overtired toddler. This killed any chance of him being adopted, so he came to Katie's Place. We set him up in a new-cat cage and warned the other volunteers to be careful with this cranky one.

He was a self-assured little character. Sprawled in his cage, he watched all the goings-on with bright-eyed interest. If you waved a toy, he responded instantly, grabbing at the dangling bauble. He loved attention and regaled us with conversational meows in his nasal squeak. But he could change in an instant from cheerful and chatty to fidgety and irritated.

He chafed at confinement, so we let him loose in the largest communal room, the Main Pen, as soon as we could. Cleaning a cage containing a cooped-up Skittles was nearly impossible. He wasn't mean, he was more like an undisciplined child. Cats and volunteers grew nervous at his blustering when he got annoyed. Whenever visitors entered the Main Pen, we looked around for Skittles, warning them, "be careful of that one." Skittles, meanwhile, might sidle over to them, beaming and angling for attention, making liars out of us. He reveled in a few pats. But if another cat crowded him, anyone within range would get an impulsive swat. Yet he was so innocently obnoxious, you couldn't help liking him.

For the volunteers who cleaned around him, he was a concern. He was bright, comical and playful. But when a big cat like Skittles vented irritation without holding back, he could draw blood. A few cleaners began to complain. One swore that he stalked her as she worked. If anything, he was probably stalking the broom that swished back and forth enticingly. Skittles didn't have a spiteful bone in his body. However, when his claws intercepted a hand or ankle, his motive didn't matter. We tried some calming medication to see if that would help. The meds had little effect, and there was nowhere else to put him.

He was also a problem for the volunteers who assigned new cats to different areas. All we needed in the Main Pen was another large, dominant male; any conflict would be ugly. Predicting feline relationships is difficult though. Skittles actually made friends with a couple of other big males, such as Grant, a former street cat who was unpredictable at times too. We would arrive to find Skittles and Grant snoozing together. When Grant was adopted, Happy Gilmore became Skittles's new best friend. Happy was a somber cat who was nervous around people. He and Skittles liked curling up in the armchair they claimed for their afternoon siestas.

When Skittles was in a good mood, life in the pen was serene. When he was in a bad mood, he stomped around mumbling and grumbling and taking swipes at anyone he passed. His roommates knew this was a really bad time to find themselves in Skittles's view. He acted without thinking, responding to a mental itch he couldn't scratch. So when his eyes fell on some unfortunate cat with a certain intensity in his gaze, we could see the other cat thinking uh-oh before hightailing it into hiding. What set him off, we never knew. One of us had a theory that newcomers triggered his mood change. Another thought the scent of an intact male before altering is what did it.

The communal room was too small and there were too many cats for him. We tried to find an adopter, but nobody wanted to take this character on. Then in early spring 2008, we sent three feral cats to a property in the countryside where they had an enclosed barn to call home. It was idyllic for cats that needed their freedom, and the more we thought about it, the more we thought Skittles might fit in there. The volunteers who cleaned were tired of his moods, the other cats were stressed, and Skittles seemed to become more restless as the months in confinement piled up.

We went to the property owner and described the big fellow, asking if she might be interested in him as a cat who could come into her home while living initially in the barn. She agreed to take him. So on May 10, 2008, a volunteer loaded Skittles into a carrier and took him to the property. The lady told us she'd looked forward to getting him. The feral cats who had preceded him were still confined in the barn to bond with the place, and they were doing well.

We were sure he'd be happy. He would have access to the outdoors. Ordinarily, we want our animals to be adopted as indoor pets. It's just plain safer. But there are some cats who cannot settle without more freedom. The barn had a cat door which locked to keep out unauthorized critters. A type of key on the cat's collar would open it when he approached the door.

The other cats in the Main Pen breathed a sigh of relief that day. Lovable as Skittles could be, the tension in that room disappeared the day he left. We wished this boisterous bounder all happiness and a good life far from the shelter.

The Many Loves of Amelia

Amelia was trapped in September 2004 as a feral youngster, three or four months old. A belligerent brown tabby, she had a lot of spunk when confronted through the cage wire by the large, noisy creatures that held her captive. But her spunk crumbled, and she flitted away in alarm if we opened the door to touch her. She shared her cage with another young feral named Adam. The two of them were already too old to socialize. No new families would cuddle these kittens. Amelia stood defiantly beside her mild-mannered roommate and watched to see what we'd do next. She met the world with her chin out as though saying take me on if you dare! She would not submit to these humans and reserved her affection for her pal Adam. They spent their time curled up in their nest where she groomed him like a protective older sister.

When it was time to release them into a communal room, they made new feline friends and depended less on each other. They stayed out of reach whenever humans were in the room. Other cats were their world, and

Amelia made friends among them easily. We've seen that semi-ferals bond with other semi-ferals while former house pets give their love to people. But relationships between animals are as complex and unpredictable as between humans. In late spring 2005, we took in a large, meek, orange-and-white street cat. Forrest had been a pet once but had been homeless for some time. He was grateful for kindness and glowed with pleasure when we gave him a fuss. We put him into Amelia's communal room, and after a while we noticed that Amelia and Forrest were often together. A strong bond formed between them and they could always be seen napping entwined, their heads tucked into each other's shoulder.

Over the months, Amelia began to appreciate human company more. She joined the other cats in asking for attention, and she began to take pleasure in a caress. She and Forrest were still a devoted couple. Clearly they would have to be adopted together. With Amelia's changing attitude toward us, finding a home for this pair no longer seemed like such a long shot.

Sure enough, in the early spring of 2006, a couple came by one Saturday and were delighted by the two cats. Forrest and Amelia's bond touched their hearts, and both cats responded to them. They expressed serious interest in adopting them. This was the first inquiry we ever had about Amelia. She was always so standoffish that people ignored her. Now, as she circled the visitors' legs and beamed up at them, it was hard to remember that she had been feral. We explained both cats' history to the couple and they went ahead with the adoption.

Amelia would need time to adjust, but with Forrest by her side, she would be fine.

Forrest settled quickly in his new life. He was pleased to have a proper home again. Predictably, Amelia was a displaced soul who hid from her new family. Sometimes she followed Forrest around like a lost

Amelia with Forrest

puppy, but mostly she stayed out of sight. Meanwhile, Forrest was thriving. He returned to the life of a house pet and embraced a relationship with his new humans while Amelia only wanted a relationship with him. After a few weeks, they brought her back to the shelter alone. We were disappointed that they couldn't give her more time. Some volunteers were upset that she was returned without Forrest. Others felt that he shouldn't lose a home where he was happy and loved. Younger and more out-going cats than Forrest were still waiting for a chance.

We returned Amelia to her communal room where she fit back in without missing a beat. If she remembered Forrest, she didn't show it. She became part of a small and close-knit group which included Adam, her first friend at the shelter; Julius and Mandarin who arrived together; and Mason, another feral youngster. She seemed to idolize Julius who was the top cat in their group. She attached herself to him, nuzzling his shoulder when he paused in his perambulations, and curling up to sleep nestled into him. Once again, she became friendly with us too. The cats greeted us together, and when Amelia wasn't nuzzling Julius she was circling our legs. Visitors inquired about her but we never found anyone who was up to dealing with her particular needs. So she carried on in her world and was content.

People frequently brought treats and Amelia's weight crept up. The cats always acted as though they were treat-deprived, but some showed the results of overindulgence. We asked people to play with them rather than bring treats. One volunteer brought a laser pointer and danced the beam over the floor. The cats ran after it in a disorganized herd, then stopped and looked nonplused when the beam disappeared.

In November 2007, Julius and Mandarin were adopted after waiting nearly three years. Now we often saw Amelia with a young, semi-feral tabby named Chivas who arrived with his mother and sister in 2006. Chivas grew up at the shelter, unable to accept human touch. Yet he was an outgoing imp who wanted to be in the middle of things. He would dance around us nuzzling everything and everyone when we visited the room. Amelia was the senior cat now, and their relationship began with Chivas idolizing her. She returned his affection, and this new bonded pair wandered the room glued to each other's side.

Chivas and Amelia both enjoyed our attention, but with their feral background they would need an understanding home. So we were pleased when, in August 2008, one of our own volunteers decided to take the pair home. She knew better than most what to expect from these cats. Amelia had never spent more than a few weeks of her four years outside the shelter, and Chivas had no experience at all with a real home. But they had each other and a patient new family.

The volunteer adored her two new cats and reported their progress to us with pride. "They are lying low behind the couch for now, but both let us give lots of pats, and Amelia is all about getting her belly rubbed. Both of them relaxed enough last night to give up some purrs which was music to our ears." She took photos and sent them to us, saying, "Doesn't it just warm your heart to see these two pals so content with each other. It is a bit hard to tell where one cat ends and the other starts. They are full of purrs, and their love for nuzzling each other is perhaps only a wee bit stronger than their love for a good belly rub."

A Shelter Pet's Catch-22

Saturn was a sturdy orange tabby with a chubby face and intelligent eyes. She had been homeless for at least six months before coming to the municipal shelter in July 2007. The person who turned her in had been watching out for her. She seemed glad to be among people again, and she was cheerful and responsive at first. However, her disposition deteriorated with confinement until the staff decided she should be sent to us.

At Katie's Place, she chose to melt into the corners of her communal room where she was never noticed. She grew impatient with too much attention; even the person who had turned her in noted that she could show a contrary streak. Aloof and independent, she preferred to be left alone. Yet she seemed to become depressed over the next months. If adopters had not been attracted to the indifferent cat in the corner before, they were certainly not interested in the cat with mucky eyes and unkempt coat that she became.

She grew finicky about food and lost weight. Treats made her perk up, and she could be tempted with plates of Fancy Feast. But without our prompting, she didn't bother to eat. We had her checked by the vet. There was nothing physically wrong. She was just unhappy at the shelter. At eight years of age, Saturn, with her dull eyes and shabby appearance, was not a prime candidate for adoption among the young, pretty cats that clamoured for attention.

The longer she was unhappy, the shabbier she let herself become, and the less likely she was to be adopted. It's a common irony at shelters that the more unhappy an animal is with shelter life, the lower her chances are of getting out. For many, it's a grim, down-hill slide with a bleak ending. We didn't know what to do with Saturn. She didn't enjoy the company of other cats. Her roommates learned fast and gave her wide berth. She didn't want human attention and became cranky if we tried to pet her. A feral colony wouldn't be good for this cat either. We noted in her description on the web that she had grown depressed and hoped to hear from someone who was moved by her plight. We couldn't promise she would become loving with a new family. At best, we expected she would be an undemanding companion and a low-maintenance pet.

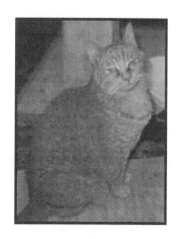

She had been at the shelter for one month short of a year when one of our volunteers took pity on her and decided to take her home. An e-mail to the volunteer group that weekend notified everyone that one of us was adopting her "to see how Miss Cranky Pants would do in a real home." The volunteer had a large house, and we thought that she would at least appreciate the chance to be alone more.

She had only been home for a short while when her new person responded to the e-mail that was sent to the group. "Cranky Pants? Did you call our sweet, rolling-on-the-floor, purring-away, letting-us-brush-her, and talking-to-us cat a Cranky Pants? Shame! She will be proud to show you how much she loves being in a home and is even respectful and friendly toward the other cats. (Yes! Do you believe it?) And she just sat in her carrier on the way here, not a word, and when she arrived, she jumped out of the carrier, no hesitation, and proceeded to rub against us, purring and purring as if to say thanks for taking me home, shelter life was just not for me. She runs to greet us, sits by my desk while I am working, and she is already figuring out that our bed is her bed too! Just a hoot, and I must say, I would have never imagined such a transformation."

We shouldn't have been surprised. We had seen cases before of animals that did a complete turnaround once they were in a home environment. But we had never seen the light-hearted, loving side of Saturn, even when she was new in shelter care and not yet depressed.

As the volunteer who adopted her said, her angels were with her. Saturn needed a real home in order to show her true nature. A compassionate gesture gave her the chance. Being at home brought out her cheerful, affectionate personality, the kind of personality adopters come to find.

The Cat Who Couldn't Identify With Cats

Chi Chi was young, healthy, pretty and friendly. But she suffered from a common and deadly syndrome among shelter cats. If they have never lived with other cats, or prefer being an only cat, they have a terrible time adjusting to shelter life. They live in a state of heightened tension which makes them edgy and even explosive although they would be calm and cheerful in conditions more natural to them. Many such cats don't make in it shelter care, and their loving side never gets a chance to show again after they lose their homes.

Chi Chi's family left her at the municipal shelter in March 2006 at the age of two and a half years. She was a feisty, opinionated tortoiseshell and, among the other cats, she had a short fuse. Then summer came with litters of kittens, each needing its own home. Summers are bad for homeless adult cats, particularly when they have attitude. Nobody wanted the temperamental tortie, so she came to Katie's Place.

She made herself at home in a communal room as well as she could and favoured a nest at shoulder level by the door where she could greet visitors and keep an eye on everything. She wanted to be queen of her realm, and she said unflattering things to new cats who joined 'her' room. Yet she was brimming with affection for people and yearned to be loved. We couldn't give her as much human company as she needed. Chi Chi was an island alone in a sea of cats.

She reached out for us and licked our hands. She climbed into our arms and nestled against us. However, within a couple of minutes, she would grow agitated and smack us or even bite. The precipitating cause would be something as simple as a cat lurking in her peripheral vision. But the effect was always the same. She took it out on whoever was closest, and she could leave you wiping a bit of blood from a scratched hand. Yet here was a cat who just wanted to cuddle.

She needed to know where all the other cats were in relation to her personal space. If she felt threatened by some movement just out of view and lost her composure, visitors assumed she was rejecting them. She didn't have the right surroundings to put her best paw forward.

The months passed, and Chi Chi adjusted, becoming less volatile, at least in the sense of being hypersensitive. She was still irritable since shelter life was not compatible with her nature. When we left her alone, she was calm, and she became reconciled to being left alone. She didn't beg for affection as she once had. She found diversion in the other cats with whom she'd never been able relate as her own kind.

To Chi Chi, they were alien beings to be toyed with or run off. One older cat was too intimidated to leave her own corner of the room after Chi Chi put the run on her a couple of times. Since we had little hope of finding a home for Chi Chi any time soon, we concentrated on finding a home for old Cheetos and, luckily, we succeeded.

Chi Chi made sport of the other cats, and her mischievous streak became apparent in her games with them. The games were more like practical jokes, and her roommates were the victims. One Saturday, we left an empty box in the pen for the cats to play with. Chi Chi hid inside it and peered through the holes, watching for another cat to wander close enough. Then she leapt out, scaring the heck out of them. She watched with delight as they dashed away, and then went back into the box to wait for another victim.

At the end of 2008, Chi Chi moved with us to the new shelter we built. She had been in shelter care for more than half her life and had adjusted as well as a temperamental cat could. She'd become a quiet resident who kept to herself most of the time. Even the other cats could forget she was there. Now, new surroundings seemed to give her new zest. We saw her playing with the pine pellets we used for their litter pans. She pranced and capered after a single pellet like a kitten.

She still had her wicked sense of mischief. One morning, she made a game out of sitting by the cat doors to the porch and leaping forward to whack the backside of any cat exiting the room. This parting shot hastened their departure considerably, to her amusement.

Chi Chi seemed happier than she'd been for some time. Maybe it was just a change of scenery she needed. The new environment worked for her. She began to enjoy attention for longer periods without getting overstimulated. Who knows how long that might have lasted. As luck would have it, we didn't get to find out.

In early January, a couple of months after moving to the new shelter and nearly three years after arriving in shelter care, Chi Chi was adopted. A family came by one Saturday looking for a cat that was a bit of a challenge. We introduced them to Chi Chi. They were confident they could handle her feisty, mischievous nature. This was the opportunity she had needed for a long time. She would have lots of space and human company, and she would be the only cat. We were pleased to see her adopted at last. But we were probably not as pleased as the cats who had been the victims of her practical jokes.

Conclusion

Over the years, Katie's Place has rescued thousands of animals, and each one has a story to tell. The stories told here describe a mere fraction of the amazing souls we've come to know. They've changed our lives as much as we've changed theirs. Each one reinforces our drive to help them in any way we can. We hope our shelter can serve as an example of what can be done when hopeless cases are given a chance to hope again. But sheltering is not the answer to the crisis of unwanted animals.

Only a changed perception of their worth will end the crisis. We rescuers need to show people what the animals have shown us. We hope that by telling their stories, we might help them. We hope that long after we're gone, people will remember the days when there were pounds full of unwanted animals and feel the same horror we feel now at the memory of workhouses or penal colonies. We hope we have contributed to the concept that animals deserve consideration simply because they live and feel.

Glossary

Barn Cat - the rare Katie's Place cat who, by reason of
   health or temperament, could not live with other
   cats and lived in the common areas of the shelter.

cat flu - a common illness among cats, particularly in
   stressful times when their immune systems can't
   work at peak efficiency. The term includes a
   number of upper respiratory viruses that produce
   runny nose, cough, sneezing, weepy eyes, lethargy
   and depressed appetite, and in severe cases, ulcers
   of eyes and mouth. (Also known as URI (upper
   respiratory infections.)

Cerebellar Hypoplasia - if a cat has feline distemper
   during pregnancy, this can affect a kitten's development so he cannot control his movements. The
   condition may be as mild as a chronic head nod or
   as severe as the inability to stand up for long.
   They are in no pain, will have a normal life span,
   and can live happily.

condo - the name used at Katie's Place for their larger
   version of a cage.

Fatty Liver Syndrome - (a.k.a. Hepatic Lipidosis) when a
   cat stops eating for more than a few days, fats
   accumulate in the liver until eventually the cat's
   skin turns yellow as the liver fails. It is fatal. The
   condition can be reversed if caught in time.

feral - abandoned, unaltered pets produce offspring
which grow up wild if they have no human contact before they are a few months old.

feral colony - occur naturally when abandoned cats
reproduce until many cats live together in the
same area. Rescuers trap, alter and release them
back to the colony if property owners/neighbours
are agreeable. This controls and eventually re-
duces the colony size. Feeding stations are maintained.

Katie - the cat who lived in the barn that was the first
Katie's Place shelter. She belonged to the barn's
owners. The shelter was named for her. She
passed away in 2006.

permanent foster - a Katie's Place arrangement wherein
an animal goes to a new home for life while the
shelter retains responsibility for the animal's vet
bills as long as the foster home uses our vets.

semi-feral - a cat who has had limited contact with humans after being born outside of a human home.
He will accept being touched although he won't
allow himself to be picked up.

upper respiratory infection - see cat flu.

Feline Leukemia (FeLV) and Feline Immunodeficiency Virus (FIV)

What are these illnesses?

Viruses that damage a cat's immune system making it susceptible to illness.

What are the symptoms?

If a cat has had several illnesses, suspect Feline Leukemia or FIV. Otherwise, they are as happy and hearty as any other cat.

How are they spread?

Feline Leukemia is spread by saliva, mucus, blood, urine. Mutual grooming, biting/fighting, sneezing, sharing bowls and litter pans *can* spread it. Prolonged, extensive cat-to-cat contact is required since the virus dies quickly with warmth and drying.

FIV is spread mainly by biting during fighting, and possibly by sharing food and water and by mutual grooming, but risk of transmission via these routes is low.

Are there vaccines for them?

Yes. They should protect your cat seven to eight out of every ten times it's exposed. (No vaccine is one hundred percent effective.)

Are they contagious to humans or other animals?

No, the viruses are species-specific which means they only affect cats.

How long will a cat survive?

Depending on the infections it's weathered, several months to several years for cats with FIV. Most cats with Feline Leukemia don't live beyond four years.

What's the treatment?

Prompt, effective management of secondary infections is the most important. Otherwise, keep the cat from being stressed (changes to the routine or the environment).

How soon can you adopt a new cat after having a cat with one or both of these viruses?

The viruses themselves only survive a few hours outside the cat. But in case the cat had any secondary infections, clean with a solution of 4 ounces of bleach to 1 gallon of water (120 ml bleach to 4 liters of water). (Thoroughly scrub food and water bowls and litter pan with this solution or discard them.) Then wait 7 to 30 days to be sure any remaining bugs die.

I am the voice of the voiceless:
Through me, the dumb shall speak;
Till the deaf world's ear be made to hear
The cry of the wordless weak.

And I am my brother's keeper,
And I will fight his fight,
And speak the word for beast and bird,
Till the world shall set things right.

- Ella Wheeler Wilcox

7275400R0

Made in the USA
Charleston, SC
11 February 2011